Forest Resources of
East Oklahoma, 2008

Richard A. Harper and
Tony G. Johnson

United States
Department of
Agriculture

Forest Service

Southern
Research Station

Resource Bulletin
SRS-187

Richard A. Harper is a Forester and Forest Resource Analyst with the Forest Inventory and Analysis Research Work Unit, Southern Research Station, U.S. Department of Agriculture Forest Service, Clemson, SC 29634.

Tony G. Johnson is a Resource Analyst (now retired), with the Forest Inventory and Analysis Research Work Unit, Southern Research Station, U.S. Department of Agriculture Forest Service, Asheville, NC 28804.

Front cover: top left, fall colors reflected, southeast Oklahoma. (photo by Darryl Hunkapillar, Oklahoma Forestry Services); top right, overlook from Robbers Cave State Park, Latimer County. (photo by Linda Doss, Oklahoma Forestry Services); bottom, rock and forests near Daisy, Pushmataha County. (photo by Kurt Atkinson, Oklahoma Forestry Services). Back cover: top left, pristine stream surrounded by a diverse forest in McCurtain County. (photo by Darryl Hunkapillar, Oklahoma Forestry Services); top right, fall colors reflected, southeast Oklahoma. (photo by Darryl Hunkapillar, Oklahoma Forestry Services); bottom, a load of logs from McCurtain County. (photo by Al Myatt, Oklahoma Forestry Services).

Unique rock outcrop appears balanced on a point, Pushmataha County, OK. (photo by Chris Joslin, Oklahoma Forestry Services)

Forest Resources of
East Oklahoma, 2008

Richard A. Harper and
Tony G. Johnson

Maintenance of forest roads
protects water quality.
(photo by Richard Harper,
Southern Research Station)

George Geissler

Robert L. Doudrick

Often thought of only as a prairie State, many people are surprised that almost 23 percent of Oklahoma is forested. Our State's forest lands are among the most diverse in the Nation; ranging from the dense pine and hardwood stands of eastern Oklahoma, through the unique Cross Timbers of the central counties, to the riparian forests of our western rivers.

Our forests have changed dramatically since the first European settlers arrived here in the 1800s and continue to change, being influenced by man's activities, natural events and long-term subtle changes in growing conditions. To ensure that all Oklahomans continue to realize the many benefits provided by their forests, we must have information we can use to assess the condition of this invaluable natural resource and determine where and how it is changing.

Starting in 1936, the U.S. Forest Service has tracked changes in the composition, extent and condition of the forest land found in the 18 eastern counties of Oklahoma through the Forest Inventory and Analysis (FIA) Program. These inventories are used by a wide variety of people, including policymakers, foresters, landowners, loggers, the forest products industry and researchers, to help them make informed decisions on the use of our forests. FIA data is also invaluable for the State's citizens to learn more about the forests around them.

In 1998, the Forest Service began partnering with State Foresters to conduct the inventory, although Oklahoma's FIA partnership with the Southern Research Station did not begin until 2006. This partnership has improved the forest inventory of Oklahoma significantly, not only providing more timely collection of data and greater input into program direction, but the expansion of the inventory to cover the entire State for the first time in our history.

This report displays the results of the seventh forest inventory of east Oklahoma and the first inventory completed in full cooperation between the Forest Service and Oklahoma Forestry Services. It presents current and accurate statistics on our forest resources, and characterizes impacts on forest health and condition from recent man-caused and natural disturbances, and changing ownership in the State.

It is with great pride that we present this report, a direct result of the strong partnership between our two agencies. We remain committed to producing the best and most useful information about the forests of Oklahoma - now and in the future.

George Geissler
State Forester and Director-Forestry Services
Oklahoma Department of Agriculture, Food and Forestry

Robert L. Doudrick
Director, Southern Research Station,
U.S. Forest Service

Foreword

This resource bulletin describes the principal findings of the seventh inventory of the forest resources in east Oklahoma. Data on the extent, condition, and classification of forest land and associated timber volumes, growth, removals, and mortality are described and interpreted.

To provide more frequent and nationally consistent information on the forest resources of the United States, the Agriculture Research Extension and Education Reform Act of 1998 (Farm Bill) authorized a change from periodic to annual surveys. These surveys are part of a continuing nationwide undertaking by the regional experiment stations of the Forest Service, U.S. Department of Agriculture (Bechtold and Patterson 2005, U.S. Department of Agriculture Forest Service 1992). Inventories of the 13 Southern States (Alabama, Arkansas, Florida, Georgia, Kentucky, Louisiana, Mississippi, North Carolina, Oklahoma, South Carolina, Tennessee, Texas, and Virginia), the Commonwealth of Puerto Rico, and the U.S. Virgin Islands are conducted by the Southern Research Station (SRS), Forest Inventory and Analysis (FIA) Research Work Unit operating from headquarters in Knoxville, TN with offices in Asheville, NC, and Starkville, MS, and with satellite facilities throughout the South.

The primary objective of these surveys is to inventory and evaluate all forest and related resources annually, providing multiresource data that serves as a basis for the formulation of forest policies and programs, strategic planning, research, and stewardship. The information presented is applicable at the State and unit level; it furnishes the background for intensive studies of critical situations, but is not designed to reflect conditions at very small scales. More information about Forest Service resource inventories is available in "Forest Service Resource Inventories:

An Overview" (U.S. Department of Agriculture Forest Service 1992). More detailed information about new sampling methodologies employed in annual FIA inventories can be found in "The Enhanced Forest Inventory and Analysis Program—National Sampling Design and Estimation Procedures" (Bechtold and Patterson 2005).

Field work began on the seventh survey of east Oklahoma in October 2007 and was completed in January 2009. Six previous surveys—completed in 1936, 1956, 1966, 1976, 1986, and 1992—provide statistics for measuring changes and trends over the past 72 years. This report primarily emphasizes changes in recent years and their implication for the forests of east Oklahoma.

White oak seedling. (photo courtesy of Oklahoma Forestry Services)

Tabular data for the FIA reports are designed to provide a comprehensive array of forest resource statistics. The 35 core tables that complement this report are found in the appendix A and can be downloaded from http://srsfia2. fs.fed.us/states/oklahoma.shtml.

Additional data for those seeking specialized information for other Southern States are available at http://srsfia2.fs.fed.us/.

Online data query tools for specific locations, landowner survey results, timber output trends, and estimates of carbon and biomass are available at http://www.fia. fs.fed.us/tools-data/other/default.asp.

Additional information about any aspect of southern forest surveys may be obtained from:

Forest Inventory and Analysis
Southern Research Station
4700 Old Kingston Pike
Knoxville, TN 37919
Telephone: 865-862-2000
William G. Burkman
Program Manager

Overlook from Robbers Cave State Park, Latimer County. (photo by Linda Doss, Oklahoma Forestry Services)

Acknowledgments

The authors gratefully acknowledge the collaboration of our colleagues from the Oklahoma Forestry Services, the excellent contributions provided by the Mississippi Forestry Commission and the Rocky Mountain and Southern Station FIA staff (including the support of Data Collection, Information Management, and Publication Management groups).

The authors would like to thank Dr. James F. Rosson, who provided great assistance regarding the history of FIA data collection methodology and processing of east Oklahoma data, and Kurt Atkinson, Dr. Kevin Hoyt, and Roger C. Conner who provided constructive reviews and comments for this report.

We would also like to acknowledge the leadership of Anne Jenkins and contributions of the publications staff: Sharon Johnson, Janet Griffin, and Charlene Walker. Their tireless efforts in checking, cross-checking, and formatting of tables, graphs, text, and layout was gratefully appreciated.

And finally, this report would not have been possible without the cooperation of private landowners who provided access to measurement plots.

Data Collection Personnel

The following people were responsible for collection of field data:

Oklahoma Forestry Services

Carri Abner
Kerry Dooley, (Former FIA Coordinator)
Matthew Woolley

Mississippi Forestry Commission

Tempel Blansett
Michael Crabb
Scott Jackson
Berry Thomas

SRS-FIA

James Brown
Mike Carr
Eric Clark III
Bobby Claybrook
Jamie Cochran
Sarah Combs
Jason Cooper
Ryan David
Lyndell Davidson
Joseph DiModica III
Andrew Edwards
Vince Few

Jay Frost
Phillip Fry
Jim Gray
Kenneth Grayson
Keith Gustafson
Jason Hewitt
Ben Koontz
Richard Leveritt
Mike Maki
Rhonda Mathison
Frank McCook
Lee McCord
Amy Morgan
Kevin Norrgard
Shawn Odom
Terry Riley
Jeremy Rogers
James Schiller
John Simpson
Greg Smith
Dan Stratton
Aaron Thigpen
Kathy Tillman
David Wall
Marcus Wood

Rocky Mountain Research Station-FIA

Mike Haldeman
Joshua Holte
Nicole Lund
Michael West
Juliet Wilhelm
Kevin Yazzie

Contents

	Page
About Forest Inventory and Analysis Inventory Reports	iii
Foreword	iii
Acknowledgments	v
List of Figures	viii
List of Tables	x
Highlights from the Seventh Forest Inventory of East Oklahoma	xiv
Introduction	1
Physiography	2
Forest Area	3
Ownership	6
Forest Types	7
Forest Management Types	9
Inventory Volume	11
Softwood Inventory	11
Hardwood Inventory	16
Components of Change	19
Softwood Average Annual Net Growth, Removals, and Mortality	20
Hardwood Average Annual Net Growth, Removals, and Mortality	22
Harvest Removals, Timber Volume, and Sustainability	22
Forest Disturbance	24
Forest Management Treatments	24
Natural Disturbances	25
Timber Removals, Utilization, and Residues	26
Introduction	26
Timber Removals and Utilization	26
Timber Products	29
Mill Residue	31
Land Use Removals	32
Logging Residue	33
Potential Recoverable Logging Residue	35
Summary—Outlook for Underutilized Material	36

Contents

	Page
Literature Cited	37
Glossary	40
Appendix A—Core Tables	47
Appendix B—Inventory Methods	102
Appendix C—Data Reliability	108
Appendix D—Species List	111

Dogwood in bloom. (photo courtesy of Oklahoma Forestry Services)

Text Figures

Figure 1—Forest survey units of east Oklahoma 2

Figure 2—Physiographic regions, provinces, and sections of Oklahoma and
east Oklahoma 3

Figure 3—Forest land area by survey year and land class, east Oklahoma 4

Figure 4—Timberland land use change by survey period, east Oklahoma 5

Figure 5—Distribution of timberland ownership, east Oklahoma, 2008 6

Figure 6—Area of timberland by ownership class and survey year, east Oklahoma 7

Figure 7—Forest-type distribution on timberland, east Oklahoma, 2008 7

Figure 8—Area of timberland by forest-management type and survey unit,
east Oklahoma, 2008 10

Figure 9—Area of timberland by forest-management type and survey year,
east Oklahoma 10

Figure 10—Area of timberland and volume of timber by survey year,
east Oklahoma 11

Figure 11—Merchantable volume of softwood live trees on timberland by
2-inch diameter class and survey year, east Oklahoma. 12

Figure 12—Tree planting area from 1928–2006, east Oklahoma 13

Figure 13—Merchantable volume of softwood live trees on timberland by
5-year age class and survey year, east Oklahoma 14

Figure 14—Softwood sawtimber inventory volume on timberland by
2-inch diameter class and survey unit, east Oklahoma, 2008 15

Figure 15—Merchantable volume of hardwood live trees on timberland by
2-inch diameter class and survey year, east Oklahoma 18

Figure 16—Hardwood sawtimber inventory volume on timberland by
2-inch diameter class and survey unit, east Oklahoma, 2008 18

Figure 17—Average annual components of change for live trees by survey period,
east Oklahoma 19

Figure 18—Average annual net growth and removals for live trees compared to total
volume by survey period, east Oklahoma 19

Figure 19—Average annual net growth and removals for softwood live trees by
survey period, east Oklahoma 20

Figure 20—Percent increase or decrease relationship of average annual net growth
and removals for live trees by survey period, east Oklahoma 20

Figure 21—Average annual net growth and removals for hardwood live trees by
survey period, east Oklahoma 22

Page

Figure 22—Comparison of inventory volume (live trees) to average annual removals (growing stock) by survey year, east Oklahoma 22

Figure 23—Average area treated/disturbed annually by treatment and disturbance types, east Oklahoma, 2008 24

Figure 24—Total harvest merchandizing from the forest to mills by merchantability class and product category, east Oklahoma, 2008 28

Appendix Figures

Figure B.1—Annual inventory fixed-plot design (the P2 plot) 105

Figure B.2—Subplot and microplot layout 105

Figure B.3—Configuration of 5-point satellite sample unit (used to collect remeasurement data for growth, removals, and mortality in the 2008 survey) 107

Figure B.4—Configuration of one satellite point 107

Wild turkey in his strut. (photo courtesy of Oklahoma Forestry Services)

Page

Text Tables

Table 1—Area by land class and survey completion date, east Oklahoma 3

Table 2—Changes in area of timberland by survey unit, east Oklahoma
from 1992 to 2008 4

Table 3—Average annual volume of all-live timber removals by removals class,
species group, and source, east Oklahoma from 1993 to 2008 28

Table 4—Average annual green weight of timber removals by removals class, species
group, and source, east Oklahoma from 1993 to 2008 29

Table 5—Average annual timber removals from all sources on timberland
by product, softwood, and hardwood, east Oklahoma from 1993 to 2008 30

Table 6—Average annual timber removals from all sources on timberland by product,
softwood, and hardwood, east Oklahoma from 1993 to 2008 30

Table 7—Average annual disposal of residue at primary wood-using plants by
product, species group, and type of residue, east Oklahoma from 1993 to 2008 32

Table 8—Average annual volume of logging residue by size class, recovery potential,
east Oklahoma from 1993 to 2008 36

Appendix Tables

Table A.1—Percentage of area by land status, east Oklahoma, 2008 47

Table A.1.1—Area by survey unit and land status, east Oklahoma, 2008 48

Table A.2—Area of forest land by ownership class and land status,
east Oklahoma, 2008 48

Table A.3—Area of forest land by forest-type group and site productivity class,
east Oklahoma, 2008 49

Table A.3.1—Area of timberland by forest-type group and site productivity class,
east Oklahoma, 2008 49

Table A.4—Area of forest land by forest-type group and ownership group,
east Oklahoma, 2008 50

Table A.4.1—Area of timberland by forest-type group and ownership group,
east Oklahoma, 2008 50

Table A.5—Area of forest land by forest-type group and stand-size class,
east Oklahoma, 2008 51

Table A.6—Area of forest land by forest-type group and stand age class,
east Oklahoma, 2008 52

Table A.6.1—Area of timberland by forest-type group and stand age class,
east Oklahoma, 2008 53

Page

Table A.7—Area of forest land by forest-type group and stand origin, east Oklahoma, 2008 54

Table A.7.1—Area of timberland by forest-type group and stand origin, east Oklahoma, 2008 54

Table A.8—Area of forest land disturbed annually by forest-type group and disturbance class, east Oklahoma, 2008 55

Table A.8.1—Area of timberland disturbed annually by forest-type group and disturbance class, east Oklahoma, 2008 55

Table A.8.2—Area of forest land treated annually by forest-type group and treatment class, east Oklahoma, 2008 56

Table A.8.3—Area of timberland treated annually by forest-type group and treatment class, east Oklahoma, 2008 57

Table A.9—Area of timberland by forest-type group and stand-size class, east Oklahoma, 2008 58

Table A.10—Number of live trees on forest land by species group and diameter class, east Oklahoma, 2008 59

Table A.10.1—Number of live trees on timberland by species group and diameter class, east Oklahoma, 2008 60

Table A.11—Number of growing-stock trees on timberland by species group and diameter class, east Oklahoma, 2008 61

Table A.12—Net volume of live trees on forest land by ownership class and land status, east Oklahoma, 2008 62

Table A.13—Net volume of live trees on forest land by forest-type group and stand-size class, east Oklahoma, 2008 63

Table A.13.1—Net volume of live trees on timberland by forest-type group and stand-size class, east Oklahoma, 2008 64

Table A.14—Net volume of live trees on forest land by species group and ownership group, east Oklahoma, 2008 65

Table A.14.1—Net volume of live trees on timberland by species group and ownership group, east Oklahoma, 2008 66

Table A.15—Net volume of live trees on forest land by species group and diameter class, east Oklahoma, 2008 67

Table A.15.1—Net volume of live trees on timberland by species group and diameter class, east Oklahoma, 2008 68

Table A.16—Net volume of live trees on forest land by forest-type group and stand origin, east Oklahoma, 2008 69

Table A.16.1—Net volume of live trees on timberland by forest-type group and stand origin, east Oklahoma, 2008 70

Table A.17—Net volume of growing-stock trees on timberland by species group and diameter class, east Oklahoma, 2008 71

Table A.18—Net volume of growing-stock trees on timberland by species group and ownership group, east Oklahoma, 2008 72

Table A.19—Net volume of sawtimber trees on timberland by species group and diameter class, east Oklahoma, 2008 73

Table A.20—Net volume of sawtimber trees on timberland by species group and ownership group, east Oklahoma, 2008 74

Table A.21—Aboveground dry weight of live trees on forest land by ownership class and land status, east Oklahoma, 2008 75

Table A.21.1—Aboveground green weight of live trees on forest land by ownership class and land status, east Oklahoma, 2008 76

Table A.22—Aboveground dry weight of live trees on forest land by species group and diameter class, east Oklahoma, 2008 77

Table A.22.1—Aboveground dry weight of live trees on timberland by species group and diameter class, east Oklahoma, 2008 78

Table A.22.2—Aboveground green weight of live trees on forest land by species group and diameter class, east Oklahoma, 2008 79

Table A.22.3—Aboveground green weight of live trees on timberland by species group and diameter class, east Oklahoma, 2008 80

Table A.22.4—Merchantable dry weight of live trees on forest land by species group and diameter class, east Oklahoma, 2008 81

Table A.22.5—Merchantable dry weight of live trees on timberland by species group and diameter class, east Oklahoma, 2008 82

Table A.23—Total carbon of live trees on forest land by ownership class and land status, east Oklahoma, 2008 83

Table A.24—Average annual net growth of live trees by ownership class and land status, east Oklahoma, 2008 (1993–2008) 84

Table A.25—Average annual net growth of live trees on forest land by forest-type group and stand-size class, east Oklahoma, 2008 (1993–2008) 85

Table A.25.1—Average annual net growth of live trees on timberland by forest-type group and stand-size class, east Oklahoma, 2008 (1993–2008) 85

Table A.26—Average annual net growth of live trees on forest land by species group and ownership group, east Oklahoma, 2008 (1993–2008) 86

Table A.26.1—Average annual net growth of live trees on timberland by species group and ownership group, east Oklahoma, 2008 (1993–2008) 87

Page

Table A.27—Average annual net growth of growing-stock trees on timberland by species group and ownership group, east Oklahoma, 2008 (1993–2008) 88

Table A.27.1—Average annual net growth of sawtimber on timberland by species group and ownership group, east Oklahoma, 2008 (1993–2008) 89

Table A.28—Average annual mortality of live trees by ownership class and land status, east Oklahoma, 2008 (1993–2008) 90

Table A.29—Average annual mortality of live trees on forest land by forest-type group and stand-size class, east Oklahoma, 2008 (1993–2008) 91

Table A.29.1—Average annual mortality of live trees on timberland by forest-type group and stand-size class, east Oklahoma, 2008 (1993–2008) 91

Table A.30—Average annual mortality of live trees on forest land by species group and ownership group, east Oklahoma, 2008 (1993–2008) 92

Table A.30.1—Average annual mortality of live trees on timberland by species group and ownership group, east Oklahoma, 2008 (1993–2008) 93

Table A.31—Average annual mortality of growing-stock trees on timberland by species group and ownership group, east Oklahoma, 2008 (1993–2008) 94

Table A.31.1—Average annual mortality of sawtimber on timberland by species group and ownership group, east Oklahoma, 2008 (1993–2008) 95

Table A.32—Average annual removals of live trees by ownership class and land status, east Oklahoma, 2008 (1993–2008) 96

Table A.33—Average annual removals of live trees on forest land by forest-type group and stand-size class, east Oklahoma, 2008 (1993–2008) 97

Table A.33.1—Average annual removals of live trees on timberland by forest-type group and stand-size class, east Oklahoma, 2008 (1993–2008) 97

Table A.34—Average annual removals of live trees on forest land by species group and ownership group, east Oklahoma, 2008 (1993–2008) 98

Table A.34.1—Average annual removals of live trees on timberland by species group and ownership group, east Oklahoma, 2008 (1993–2008) 99

Table A.35—Average annual removals of growing-stock trees on timberland by species group and ownership group, east Oklahoma, 2008 (1993–2008) 100

Table A.35.1—Average annual removals of sawtimber on timberland by species group and ownership group, east Oklahoma, 2008 (1993–2008) 101

Table C.1—Statistical reliability for east Oklahoma, 2008 109

Table D.1—Common name, scientific name, and FIA species code of tree species ≥1.0 and ≤5.0 inches in d.b.h. occurring in the FIA sample, east Oklahoma, 2008 111

• Total forest land area in the 18 counties of east Oklahoma was 5.7 million acres, of which 5.1 million acres was timberland.

• Timberland area increased 18 percent or 780,000 acres since 1976.

• Since 1992, 387,000 acres of timberland were converted to other land uses, but 595,000 acres reverted to timberland with a net gain of 207,000 acres. This net gain of timberland equates to about 13,000 acres a year.

• Hardwood forest types covered 78 percent of forest land area on 4.0 million acres. Softwood forest types occupied 1.1 million acres of timberland.

• Oak-hickory was the predominate forest type with 2.9 million acres representing 57 percent of the timberland area.

• Planted pine area on timberland increased 23 percent since 1992 totaling 585,000 acres.

• The majority of timberland in east Oklahoma was owned by nonindustrial private individual forest landowners, who held 2.9 million acres or 57 percent, compared to 11 percent for forest industry and 17 percent for other corporations.

• A major shift in ownership occurred since 1992 when forest industry divested almost 469,000 or 45 percent of its land. The majority of this land changed to corporate ownership which increased 556,000 acres or 265 percent.

• Softwood and hardwood volume were at an alltime high as total volume in east Oklahoma has more than doubled since 1966.

• Since 1992, planted pine volume surged 85 percent totaling almost 630 million cubic feet. Natural pine forest-management type volume decreased 16 percent, but contains slightly more volume than planted pine with 702 million cubic feet.

• While gross growth has increased for the 2008 survey, both mortality and removals have also increased since the 1992 inventory. Net growth decreased 10 percent since 1992, but still exceeds removals and contributes to the increase in total inventory volume.

• Although harvest removals of growing stock more than tripled since 1966, the total timber inventory of live-tree volume has more than doubled (117 percent).

• About 101,900 acres experienced some type of harvesting each year of which 34,500 acres a year were a final harvest. The average annual tree planting and natural regeneration totaled 34,700 acres per year.

• Pulpwood was the leading product—accounting for 38 percent of total product output or 1.6 million green tons—followed by sawtimber with 35 percent or 1.5 million green tons.

• An estimate of the average annual logging residues totaled 14.7 green tons per acre with a potential recovery rate of about 5.7 green tons per acre.

Pristine stream surrounded by a diverse forest in McCurtain County. (photo by Darryl Hunkapillar, Oklahoma Forestry Services)

xiv

Introduction

This report presents the results of the seventh forest survey for east Oklahoma from field plots established by the Forest Inventory and Analysis (FIA) Research Unit (U.S. Department of Agriculture Forest Service, Southern Research Station). The last FIA forest survey was completed in 1992 using the variable radius plot design, i.e., data were collected on 10 points with a 37.5 basal area factor prism. The recent survey (inventory cycle 7) followed 16 years later and used an annual fixed radius design that incorporated four subplots with a 24-foot radius. Field data collection began October 2007 and ended January 2009. The cycle 7 dataset is known as east Oklahoma 2008.

Plot distribution for the fixed radius plot design developed for the new annual system of updates provided little overlap for remeasurement of the subplots that were established in 1992. Only a few trees were tallied in both the sixth and seventh inventories, resulting in a partial remeasurement. Thus, increasing timeliness of data through annual updates also means a loss of continuity in tracking tallied trees back through time.

Estimates of the components of change—known as average annual net growth, removals, and mortality—provided in this report are based on remeasurement of the 1992 plots using the variable radius inventory method. Future estimates of the components of change will be based on remeasurement of the fixed radius plots established during the seventh inventory.

Implementing the new annual inventory required switching data collection systems from a periodic type format to an annualized format where the sample plots in the full survey cycle are dispersed equally among the number of years in the cycle (currently 5 years). Another major change was a shift from forest/nonforest area estimation based upon aerial photography dot count methodology to a system that provides area estimates using stratified estimation techniques to reduce variance.

Redbud in bloom—Oklahoma State tree. (photo courtesy of Oklahoma Forestry Services)

Differences in survey design, plot distribution, variables collected, and data processing algorithms and procedures limit trend analysis to simple comparisons of tabular data from past reports or online tools. Therefore, trend data presented should be considered as a general change in the resource and not a true trend analysis.

More detailed information concerning methods and trends are provided in the methods section of the appendix.

Previous inventory cycles for east Oklahoma were completed in 1936, 1956, 1966, 1976, 1986, and 1992. All of the analytical reports for previous inventories are available online at the FIA Oklahoma Web site http://srsfia2.fs.fed.us/states/oklahoma.shtml.

A cooperative inventory effort for central and west Oklahoma was conducted in 1989 involving U.S. Department of Agriculture Forest Service, Natural Resources Conservation Service, and the Oklahoma Division of Forestry (Rosson 1995). Establishment of FIA plots began in 2009 and that effort is projected to be complete within 10 years.

The figures and tables in this report help present the analysis of the 2008 survey data. The appendices contain the 35 core tables for the 2008 survey (appendix A), the survey methods (appendix B), data reliability considerations (appendix C), and a list of tree species sampled (appendix D). The core tables are also available on the FIA, east Oklahoma Web page at http://srsfia2.fs.fed.us/states/oklahoma.shtml.

Physiography

The 18 counties in east Oklahoma are divided into two survey units: 10 in the southeast and the remainder in the northeast (fig. 1).

Oklahoma falls within three physiographic regions—Atlantic Plain, Interior Highlands, and Interior Plains. Within these three regions are five physiographic provinces, four of which makeup the two east Oklahoma units: the Coastal Plain, the Ouachita, the Ozark Plateaus, and the Central Lowland (fig. 2) (Fenneman 1938,

Vigil and others 2000). These four provinces are divided into six sections:

1. West Gulf Coastal Plain
2. Ouachita Mountains
3. Arkansas Valley
4. Boston "Mountains"
5. Springfield-Salem plateaus
6. Osage Plains

These landforms from historical geological structure support a diverse landscape for east Oklahoma and therefore the bases of forest types and management objectives.

Figure 1—Forest survey units of east Oklahoma.

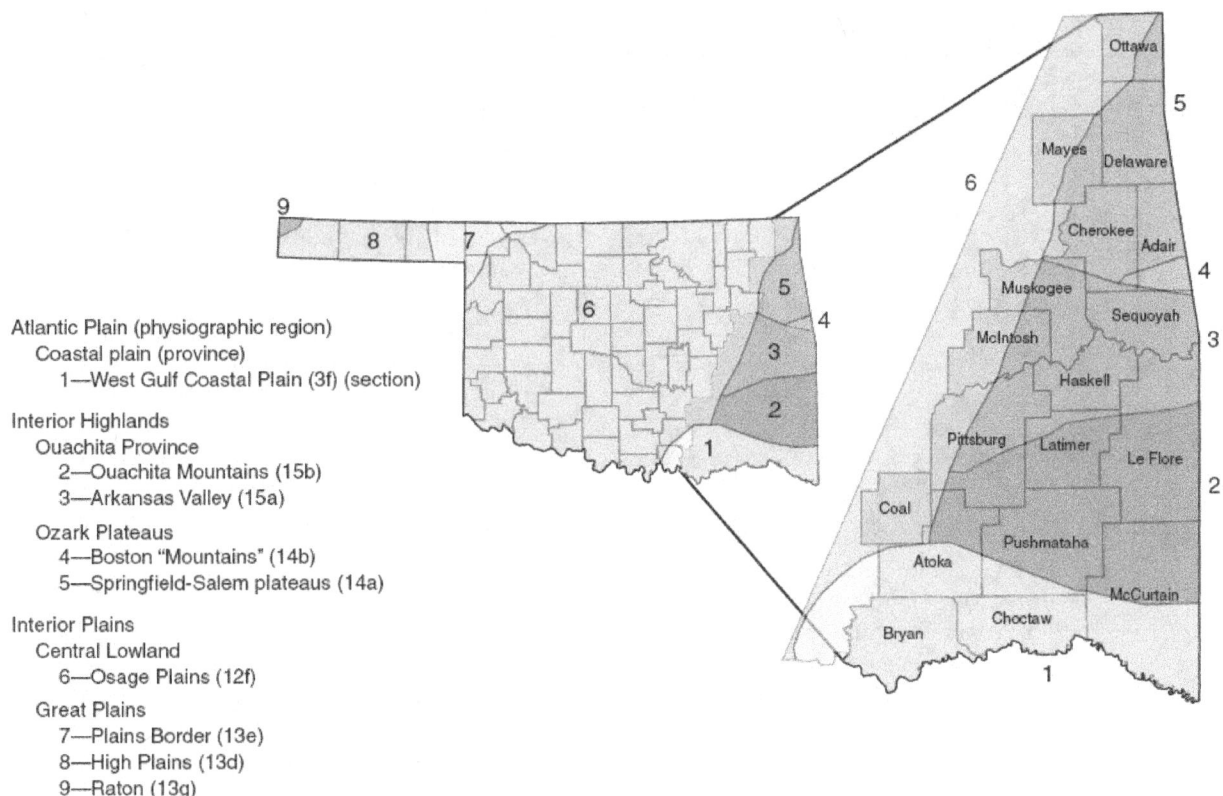

Atlantic Plain (physiographic region)
    Coastal plain (province)
        1—West Gulf Coastal Plain (3f) (section)

Interior Highlands
    Ouachita Province
        2—Ouachita Mountains (15b)
        3—Arkansas Valley (15a)

    Ozark Plateaus
        4—Boston "Mountains" (14b)
        5—Springfield-Salem plateaus (14a)

Interior Plains
    Central Lowland
        6—Osage Plains (12f)

    Great Plains
        7—Plains Border (13e)
        8—High Plains (13d)
        9—Raton (13g)

Figure 2—Physiographic regions, provinces, and sections of Oklahoma and east Oklahoma. Information acquired from USGS, A Tapestry of Time and Terrain who adapted it from Fenneman 1938. Numbers with letters in parenthesis correspond to province and section respectively, and located at the USGS Web site http://tapestry.usgs.gov/Default.html.

Forest Area

All forest land in 2008 totaled > 5.7 million acres and represented 57 percent of the 10.1 million acres of total land area in east Oklahoma (table 1). Since the mid-1970s, forest land area has increased about 818,300 acres or 17 percent (fig. 3) (Earles 1976, Hines and Bertelson 1987, Sternitzke and Van Sickle 1968). Forest land area classified as timberland (capable of growing 20 cubic feet of wood per acre annually and available for commercial harvesting) occupied 5.1 million acres in 2008. Timberland accounted for 50 percent of the total land area in east Oklahoma. Timberland area increased 207,600 acres or about 4 percent since 1992.

Table 1—Area by land class and survey completion date, east Oklahoma

Land class	Survey completion date					
	1956	1966	1976	1986	1992	2008
	million acres					
Timberland	5.63	4.82	4.32	4.75	4.90	5.10
Other/reserved	0.12	0.65	0.60	0.51	0.52	0.64
Total forest land	5.75	5.47	4.93	5.26	5.42	5.74
Nonforest land	4.05	4.19	5.19	5.30	4.69	4.39
Total land area	9.80	9.66	10.12	10.56	10.10	10.14
Percent forested	59	57	49	50	54	57

Totals may not sum due to rounding.
Total land area estimates changed slightly over time due to improvements in measurement techniques and refinements in classification of small bodies of water and streams.

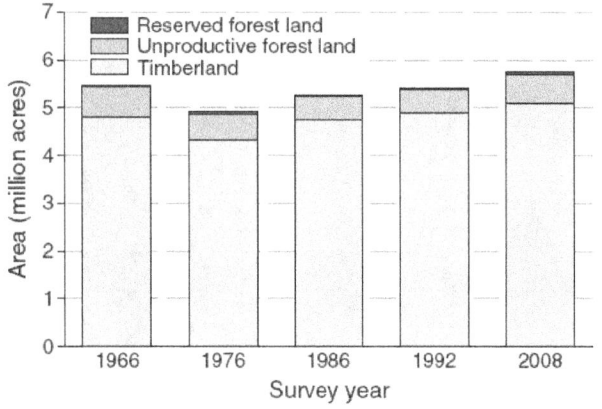

Figure 3—Forest land area by survey year and land class, east Oklahoma.

Parks, wilderness areas, historic sites, and other forest land where commercial timber harvesting is prohibited by statute are known as reserved forest land. Reserved forest land occupied 1 percent of the forest land area in east Oklahoma. Land area that is unproductive forest land (not capable of growing 20 cubic feet of wood per acre annually) accounts for 10 percent of total forest land area.

The Southeast unit, which falls primarily in the Ouachita province, includes part of the Coastal Plain province to the south and forms the east boundary of the Central Lowland province to the west. The Northeast unit is split by the Ouachita province to the south and Ozark Plateaus province to the north and also forms the east boundary of the Central Lowlands province to the west (fig. 2). The Southeast unit contained the majority of timberland area in east Oklahoma, with 3.7 million acres or 73 percent. The Northeast unit had 1.4 million acres of timberland. Both units gained about 4 percent of timberland area since the 1992 survey.

Changes in land use have shifted the location of timberland area throughout east Oklahoma. Part of this shift is the market-driven cycle of agricultural and timberland uses that swap area back and forth over time. Perhaps the greatest impact is the loss of timberland to nonforest development where deforestation occurs. Table 2 represents land use change by survey unit since 1992. Land use change was based on the remeasured plot data and provides estimates of timberland area that remained in timberland, changed from timberland to a different land use, or was converted from a nonforest land use to timberland.

Losses—The total timberland loss was 468,700 acres. About 25 percent of the loss was converted to agriculture and 14 percent was converted to development, which averaged about 4,400 acres a year. More than one-half of the total loss was to other forest land, which includes land being reclassified as reserved or unproductive forest land (fig. 4).

Table 2—Changes in area of timberland by survey unit, east Oklahoma from 1992 to 2008

Survey unit	Area of timberland			Changes							
				Additions from			Diversions to				
	1992	2008	Net change	Total gain	Non-forest	Other forest land	Total loss	Other forest land	Agri-culture	Urban and other	Water
	thousand acres										
Southeast	3,564.6	3,725.1	160.5	475.0	444.4	30.6	314.5	181.4	78.6	31.5	23.0
Northeast	1,331.2	1,378.0	46.8	201.0	195.0	6.0	154.2	69.8	37.3	37.3	10.0
Total	4,895.8	5,103.1	207.3	676.0	639.4	36.6	468.7	251.2	115.8	68.8	32.9

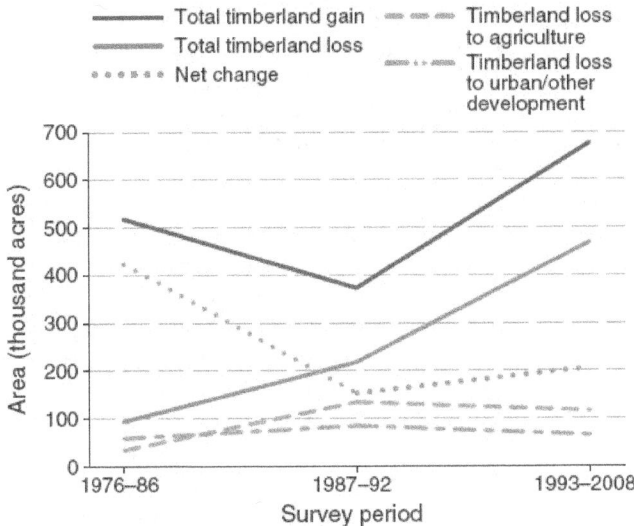

The two dashed lines added together represent the majority of total timberland loss (solid red line). However, for the 1993–2008 period, an additional 54 percent of timberland loss is due to timberland reclassified as unproductive forest land (not shown on chart).

Figure 4—Timberland land use change by survey period, east Oklahoma.

Gains—The total gain in timberland area was 676,000 acres or about 43,500 acres per year. It is estimated that 583,100 acres of agricultural land reverted back to timberland since 1992 averaging almost 37,500 acres per year. This accounted for 86 percent of the gain of timberland.

Net changes—The net change was an increase of 207,300 acres (or 13,100 acres per year) of timberland since 1992. Fortunately, east Oklahoma has experienced a period where total timberland gain exceeded timberland loss (fig. 4). However, the trend, albeit positive, is one of declining gains. From 1976 to 1986, the net change was >42,400 acres per year (Hines and Bertelson 1987), decreasing to 25,700 acres per year from 1987 to 1993 (Rosson 2001).

Human interface with forest and wildlife poses challenges for forest operations and creates limited defensible space from wildfire. (photo by Michelle Finch-Walker, Oklahoma Forestry Services)

Ownership

FIA classifies two general ownership categories: public lands and private lands (fig. 5). Within the public lands, national forest lands represented 5 percent of all timberland or 257,500 acres. Other Federal lands (including the U.S. Fish and Wildlife Service, the Departments of Defense and Energy), totaled 296,600 acres as of 2008. State owned timberland was 136,500 acres and local public land totaled 27,600 acres. All public land comprised about 14 percent of timberland area in east Oklahoma.

The remaining 86 percent of timberland ownership was held by private landowners. The majority was owned by individuals or families totaling 2.9 million acres or 57 percent. Forest industry is classified as landholdings that also operate a primary forest products mill. They represent 11 percent of all timberland or 568,300 acres.

Some nonindustry private ownerships are incorporated, such as timber investment management organizations (TIMOs), real estate investment trusts (REITs), limited liability companies, or other incorporated ownerships. Together, they held 891,300 acres or 18 percent of all timberland.

Timberland ownerships have always experienced movement from one group to another, but the majority of land transfers occurs in the private ownership category. The distribution of timberland area among private ownerships remained relatively stable until the late 1990s. Throughout the 1990s and early 2000s, market pressures, tax policy, and an abundant wood supply were catalysts for a wave of private ownership change. The vertically integrated forest industry began divesting its landholdings. Although some timberland was sold directly to individuals and other forest industry companies (Harper and others 2009), most went to nonindustrial corporate ownerships such as TIMOs or REITs with agreements to provide long-term wood supplies for the sellers' mills. Figure 6 shows the shift of timberland ownership from forest industry to corporate from 1992 to 2008. Forest industry ownership declined 45 percent (469,200 acres) and nonindustrial corporate ownership increased 265 percent (556,500 acres). Individuals and family timberland ownership experienced little change and public lands increased 24 percent. Note that much of the change in industry ownership was influenced by the land swap from Weyerhaeuser to the Ouachita National Forest.[1]

---

[1]Personal communication. 2011. K. Atkinson, Assistant Director, Oklahoma Forestry Services, Oklahoma Department of Agriculture, Food and Forestry, 2800 N. Lincoln Blvd., Oklahoma City, OK 73105.

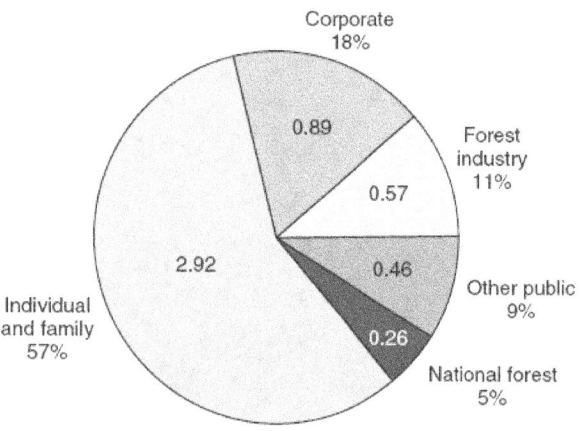

Total 5.10 million acres

Figure 5—Distribution of timberland ownership, east Oklahoma, 2008.

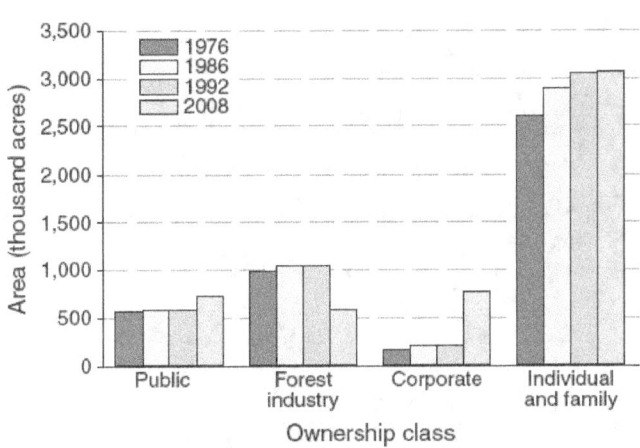

Figure 6—Area of timberland by ownership class and survey year, east Oklahoma.

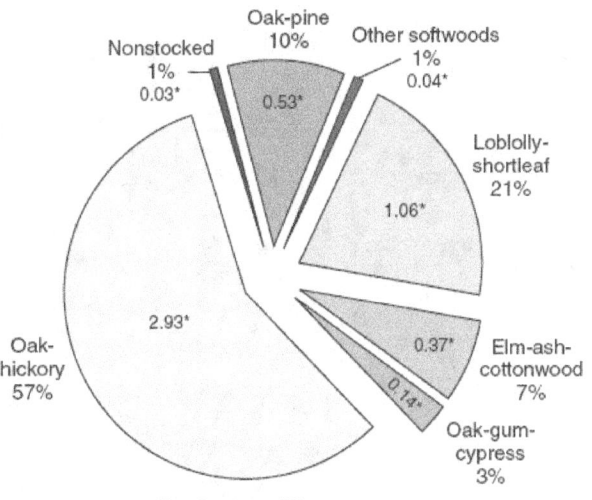

Total 5.10 million acres

*Million acres

Figure 7—Forest-type distribution on timberland, east Oklahoma, 2008.

Forest Types

Ninety-six softwood and hardwood tree species were tallied on FIA plots within the four physiographic provinces of east Oklahoma (appendix D). The percent stocking of these species on a plot determines the forest type (fig. 7). Loblolly-shortleaf pines and other softwood forest types accounted for 21 percent of the timberland or 1.1 million acres, compared to 78 percent or 4.0 million acres for hardwoods. The predominant hardwood forest types were oak-pine, oak-hickory, oak-gum-cypress, and elm-ash-cottonwood.

Fall colors reflected, southeast Oklahoma. (photo by Darryl Hunkapillar, Oklahoma Forestry Services)

Bottomland hardwoods in Little River National Wildlife Refuge, McCurtain County. (photo by Darryl Hunkapillar, Oklahoma Forestry Services)

Combined, the oak-hickory and loblolly-shortleaf forest-type groups makeup 78 percent of the timberland area in east Oklahoma.

These broad forest types are broken down into seven forest-type groups:

Softwood	Hardwood
Loblolly-shortleaf	Oak-pine
Other eastern softwoods	Oak-hickory
	Oak-gum-cypress
	Elm-ash-cottonwood
	Other hardwoods

Oak-hickory was the predominate forest-type group with 2.9 million acres representing 57 percent of the timberland area in east Oklahoma (fig. 7). It occupied 48 percent of the timberland area in the Southeast unit or 1.8 million acres and 1.1 million acres or 81 percent of the timberland area in the Northeast unit.

Loblolly-shortleaf pine was the next most abundant forest-type group occupying 21 percent of the timberland area (1.1 million acres). This forest-type group occurred primarily in the Southeast unit with >1.0 million acres representing 95 percent of the total softwood area in east Oklahoma. Only 14,500 acres were in the Northeast unit.

Oak-pine forest-type group occupied 10 percent of timberland or about 530,000 acres.

Elm-ash-cottonwood accounted for 7 percent of timberland area or 370,000 acres.

Oak-gum-cypress occupied only 3 percent of the timberland area or 141,500 acres.

The remaining forest-type groups were other eastern softwoods, which were composed mostly of eastern redcedar and occupied 40,100 acres; and other hardwoods, which occupied 8,800 acres.

Forest land stocked with <10 percent live trees is considered nonstocked. This is usually areas of timberland recently harvested and in transition to a forest type once trees are reestablished naturally or by tree planting. Less than 1 percent of the total timberland area in east Oklahoma was classified as nonstocked.

Oak-pine stand. (photo courtesy of Oklahoma Forestry Services)

Forest-Management Types

Forest-management types broadly demonstrate the influence of forest management operations on the landscape resulting in changes in forest composition (fig. 8). In 2008, east Oklahoma had >585,000 acres of planted pine, all occurring in the Southeast unit. Although tree planting has occurred since the 1930s, the practice of planting loblolly pine became more extensive in the early 1970s. By 1986, >264,000 acres of planted pine were reported, increasing to >474,000 acres by 1992. From 1986 to 2008, pine planting grew by 121 percent (fig. 9).

Since 1976, natural softwood area decreased by 40 percent from about 847,000 acres to 512,000 acres—mostly the result of regenerating harvested forests into more productive pine plantations. Some acres were converted to other land uses such as agriculture or development. Overall, total softwood area (natural and planted) has experienced a 29-percent increase or about 250,000 acres.

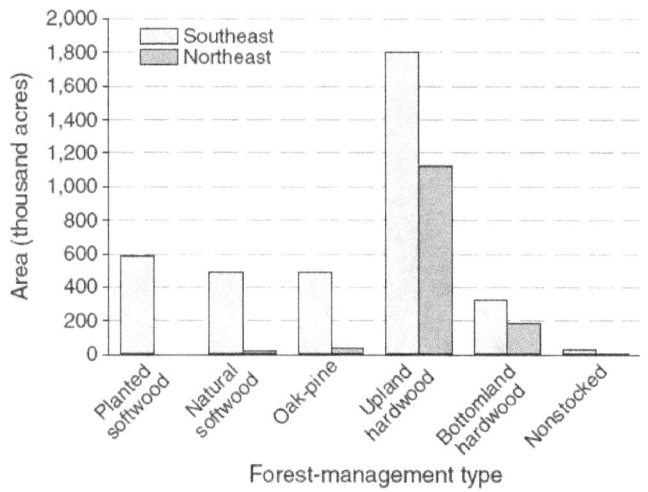

Figure 8—Area of timberland by forest-management type and survey unit, east Oklahoma, 2008.

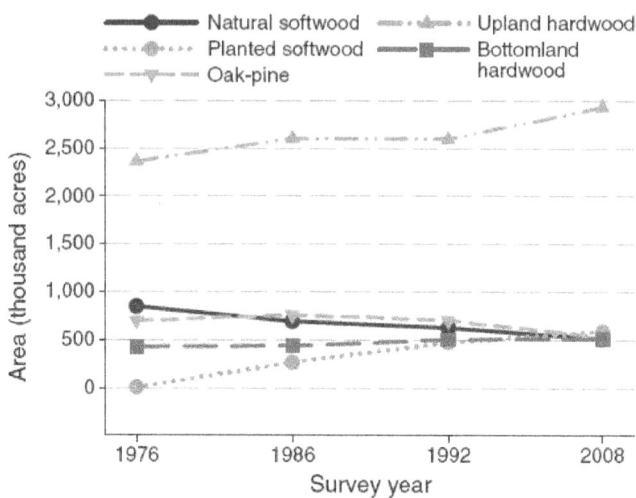

Figure 9—Area of timberland by forest-management type and survey year, east Oklahoma.

Oak-pine management type has experienced change to and from upland hardwood and softwood stands, and sometimes it is converted to planted pine after harvesting. Since 1986, oak-pine management type has declined 30 percent or 227,000 acres. Most of this decrease occurred since 1992 showing a decline of 172,000 acres or 25 percent.

The upland hardwood management type contains the largest area of 2.9 million acres.

About 339,000 acres were added since 1992, representing a 13-percent increase.

East Oklahoma had about 511,000 acres of bottomland hardwood in 2008. This management type has shown an increase of about 85,000 acres or 20 percent since 1976 and indicative of a relatively stable management type.

Inventory Volume

The change in inventory volume on timberland is primarily influenced by change in timberland area, diameter distribution, trees per acre, and application of timberland management methods (silviculture). However, volume computation methods changed for east Oklahoma 2008 and values stated may be higher than the real change in the resource (see Appendix B—Inventory Methods). Since 1966, total inventory volume of live trees in east Oklahoma has shown a steady increase totaling 2.8 billion cubic feet or almost 117 percent (fig. 10) (Sternitzke and Van Sickle 1968). This dramatic increase in inventory volume has occurred without a substantive increase in timberland area.

About three-quarters or 9,255.2 million board feet (International ¼-inch log rule) of the sawtimber volume on east Oklahoma's timberland was held by private landowners. Family or individual ownerships have 7,544.0 million board feet or 61 percent of the sawtimber volume. Since 1992, the total sawtimber volume increased 3,099.8 million board feet on all private timberland and 1,213.8 million board feet on all public land. Total sawtimber volume increased 54 percent or 4,313.5 million board feet since 1992.

Softwood Inventory

Softwood inventory volume was at an all-time high in 2008 with 1.6 billion cubic feet representing 32 percent of the total inventory in east Oklahoma. The softwood volume increased 15 percent since 1992 and 114 percent since 1966 (Sternitzke and Van Sickle 1968). Shortleaf pine was the dominate species representing 55 percent of the volume or 896 million cubic feet followed by loblolly pine with 669 million cubic feet representing 41 percent of the softwood volume. The remaining 4 percent was eastern redcedar.

Since 1992, planted pine volume surged 85 percent totaling almost 630 million cubic feet. Natural softwood forest-type volume decreased 16 percent, but continued to outpace planted pine with 702 million cubic feet.

The Southeast unit contained the majority (98 percent) of softwood volume in east Oklahoma. Shortleaf pine made-up 51 percent of the softwood volume with 840 million cubic feet. Virtually all (>99.9 percent) of the loblolly inventory volume was located in this unit.

Distribution of volume by diameter class offers some insight for future volume and figure 11 demonstrates shifts in volume by diameter class over time (Miles 2010).

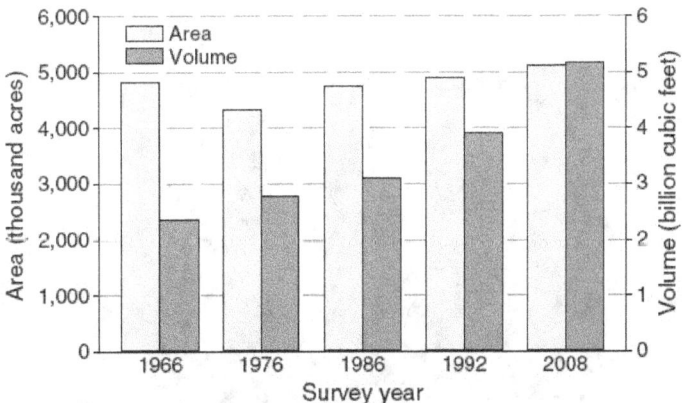

Figure 10—Area of timberland and volume of timber by survey year, east Oklahoma.

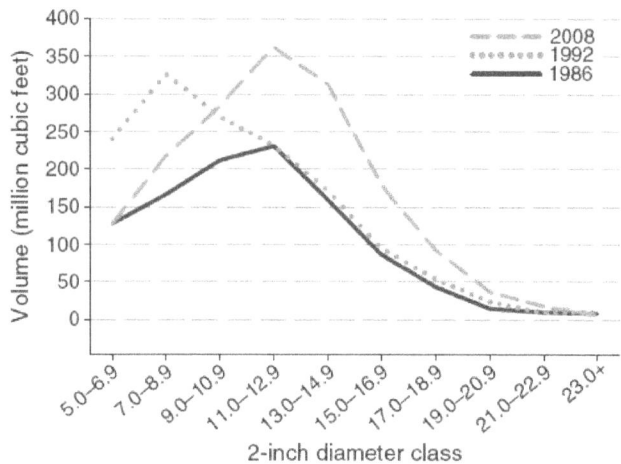

Figure 11—Merchantable volume of softwood live trees on timberland by 2-inch diameter class and survey year, east Oklahoma.

rates ranging from 30 percent to almost 149 percent.

Figure 11 demonstrates how volume shifted among diameter classes over the 22-year period. From 1986 to 1992, the peak in volume shifted from the 11-inch class to the 7-inch class. This shift resulted mostly from postharvest tree planting in the late 1970s and 1980s. By 1986, these planted stands grew to merchantable size (stand diameter ≥5-inch class) resulting in increased volume in the 7-inch class. These planted stands continued to increase in average stand diameter, resulting in a volume shift back to the 11-inch class by 2008, but with 57 percent more volume than reported in 1986.

The 55-percent increase in inventory volume since 1986 can be seen in the volume distributed across 2-inch diameter classes. In 1986, softwood volume peaked at 230 million cubic feet in the 11-inch diameter class. By 2008 the peak in the 11-inch diameter class reached 362 million cubic feet, an increase of 57 percent. With only two exceptions (the 5- and ≥23-inch classes), all diameter classes increased at

The peak in volume could continue to track toward the 13-inch class in the next survey cycle, but that outcome would depend on many factors—such as timber markets, tree planting, and natural disturbances (mainly fire, insects, disease, and weather events). However, increased demand for forest products combined with the recent decline in tree planting may deplete the volume and shift the peak back toward 1986 levels.

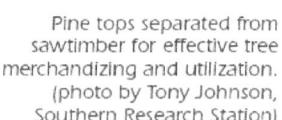

Pine tops separated from sawtimber for effective tree merchandizing and utilization. (photo by Tony Johnson, Southern Research Station)

Tree planting after harvest increases productivity of a forest. (photo by Tony Johnson, Southern Research Station)

Tree planting—Tree planting using genetically improved stock, fertilization, and herbicide applications has influenced softwood volume in east Oklahoma over the last 30 years.

Early records show tree planting began in 1928,[2,3] and reached about 136,000 acres by 1971. Over the next 35 years (1972 through 2006) >1.0 million acres had been planted (fig. 12). The increased volume from planted acres became evident in the 1992 FIA survey as the average stand diameters reached the merchantable threshold of ≥5 inches diameter at breast height (d.b.h.).

Excludes years 1938 and 1941–44.
1980 and 1981 are estimated.

Figure 12—Tree planting area from 1928–2006, east Oklahoma.

[2] U.S. Department of Agriculture, Forest Service. 2001. 2005. Historic tree planting data. [Not paged]. Unpublished data. On file with: Richard A. Harper, Southern Research Station, Forest Inventory and Analysis, 127 Lehotsky Hall, Clemson, SC 29634.

[3] Georgia Forestry Commission. 2007. Southeastern states reforestation efforts. 3 p. Unpublished data. On file with: Richard A. Harper, Southern Research Station, Forest Inventory and Analysis, 127 Lehotsky Hall, Clemson, SC 29634.

Volume by age class—Figure 13 shows the volume by 5-year age classes for natural and planted softwood trees for survey years 1986, 1992, and 2008 (Miles 2010). In 1986, the majority (99 percent) of the softwood volume was in natural stands. The 21- to 50-year age classes accounted for 724 million cubic feet or 69 percent of the total softwood volume (fig. 13a). By 1992, most of the softwood volume (937 million cubic feet or 67 percent) shifted to younger stand-age classes ranging from 11 to 30 years of age (fig. 13b).

Planted pine trees represented 25 percent of the volume in 1992 (fig. 13b). By 2008, the softwood volume by age class was split about 39 and 61 percent between planted and natural volume, respectively (fig. 13c). The transition was most evident in the 36- to 40-year age class for both management types. Planted trees represented 81 percent of the volume of the age classes <36 years, and naturally generated trees represented 94 percent of the volume in the age classes >35 years. Note that 44 percent of the total softwood volume was in age classes <36 years.

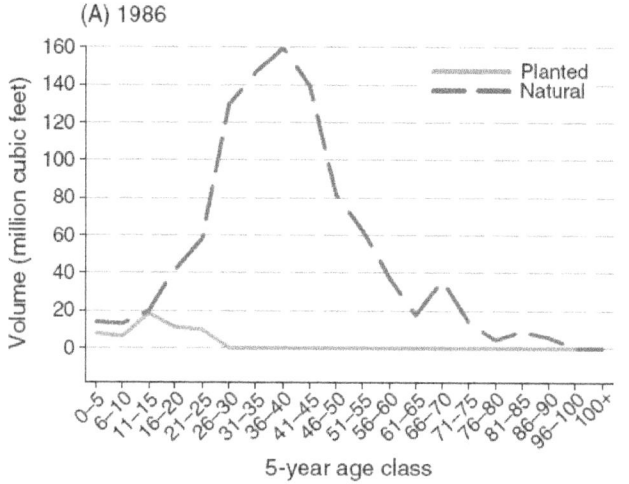

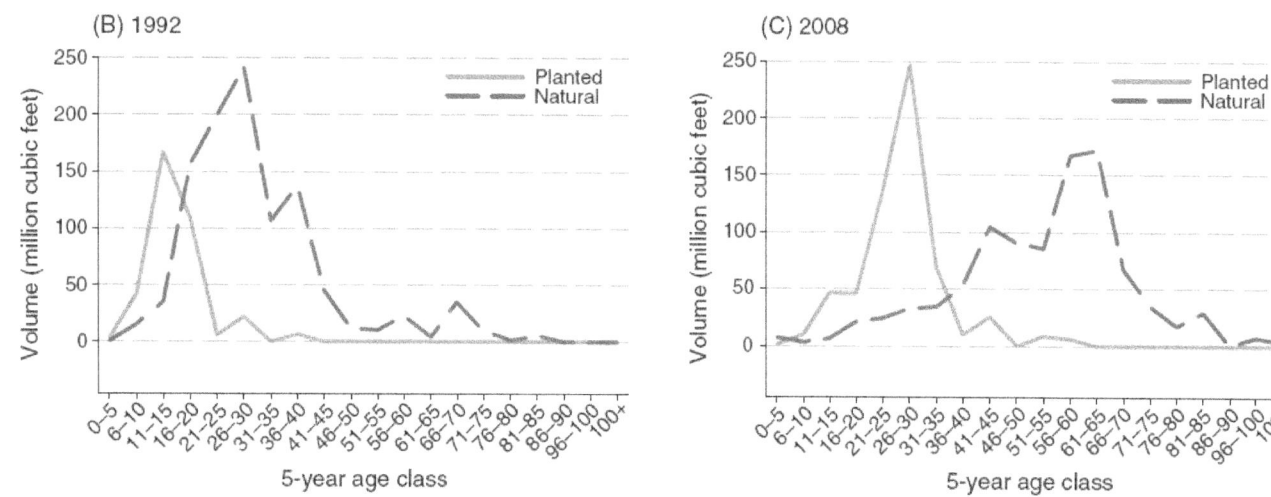

Figure 13—Merchantable volume of softwood live trees on timberland by 5-year age class and survey year, east Oklahoma (A) 1986, (B) 1992, and (C) 2008.

Sawtimber—Figure 14 shows the volume of softwood sawtimber of 2-inch diameter classes by survey unit. Softwood sawtimber volume totaled 5.9 billion board feet (International ¼-inch rule) in 2008, a 41-percent increase (1.7 billion board feet) since 1992. Eighty-eight percent of the increase was in the 11.0 to 16.9 diameter classes. Volume in the 9.0 to 10.9 diameter class declined 11 percent.

Almost 69 percent or 4,033.4 million board feet of the softwood sawtimber volume was held by private landowners. Family or individual ownerships have 2.7 billion board feet or 46 percent of the total sawtimber volume. Since 1992, sawtimber volume increased almost 1.1 billion board feet on all private timberland and 638.8 million board feet on all public land.

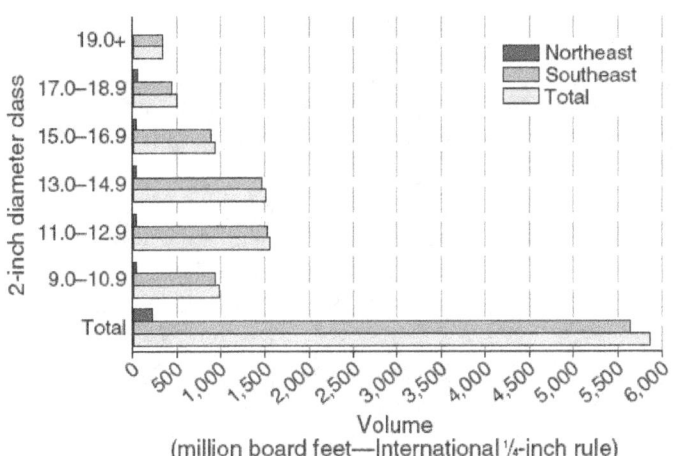

Figure 14—Softwood sawtimber inventory volume on timberland by 2-inch diameter class and survey unit, east Oklahoma, 2008.

Patterns of shade and light on wooded path. (photo by Darryl Hunkapillar, Oklahoma Forestry Services)

15

Hardwood Inventory

Hardwood inventory accounted for 68 percent of the total inventory in east Oklahoma. It has increased in every FIA survey since 1936, with the current volume of 3.5 billion cubic feet of live trees at an all time high (Eldredge and Cruikshank 1938). Hardwood inventory volume increased by 41 percent (>1.0 million cubic feet) since 1992 and more than doubled (119 percent) since 1966 (Sternitzke and Van Sickle 1968).

Unlike softwood species groups where two species dominated the volume, the hardwood inventory consisted of 76 species consolidated into 17 species groups and five forest-type groups defining the hardwood inventory. Post oak totaled the most volume with 880 million cubic feet or 25 percent of the total hardwood volume in east Oklahoma. Black oak followed with 386 million cubic feet or 11 percent of hardwood volume while white oak accounted for 270 million cubic feet and 8 percent of the volume. Combined, these three species makeup 1.5 billion cubic feet and 44 percent of the hardwood volume.

Forest cover protects water quality. (photo courtesy of Oklahoma Forestry Services)

Hardwood forests dominate the east Oklahoma landscape accounting for 77 percent of the area.
(photo courtesy of Oklahoma Forestry Services)

All three of these species form a major component of the stocking in the upland hardwood management group which consists of the oak-pine and oak-hickory forest-type groups. There were 3.1 million cubic feet of all-live volume in these two forest-type groups or almost 82 percent of the hardwood inventory.

Water oak, southern red oak, black hickory, green ash, mockernut hickory, northern red oak, winged elm, sweetgum, and blackjack oak each contained between 4 to 3 percent (listed in declining order) of the hardwood volume. Combined, they totaled >1.0 billion cubic feet or 30 percent of the hardwood volume.

Individual species are sometimes combined into species groups that relate to forest products categories. The dominant species groups ranked by volume include:

Species group	Volume
	percent
Other white oaks	26
Other red oaks	23
Hickory	11
Select white oaks	9
Ash	5
Select red oaks	5
Sweetgum	3
Soft maple	2

These eight hardwood species groups totaled 2.9 billion cubic feet or 83 percent of the hardwood volume.

The bottomland management group consists of oak-gum-cypress and elm-ash-cottonwood forest types. These forest types contain 695 million cubic feet or 18 percent of hardwood inventory.

Diameter class distribution of hardwood volume has been more stable than that for softwood. In figure 15, the 2008 data reflect the 41-percent increase in volume since 1992, discussed above, for all diameter classes except the 6-inch class, which remained relatively unchanged (Miles 2010). The greatest increase in volume occurred in the consolidated diameter classes ≥23 inches.

Hardwood volume was split between the two survey units in east Oklahoma. The Southeast unit had slightly more hardwood volume with 2.0 billion cubic feet or 57 percent. The Northeast unit had 1.5 billion cubic feet representing 43 percent of the hardwood volume.

Figure 16 shows the volume by diameter class and survey unit of hardwood sawtimber, which totaled 6.5 billion board feet (International ¼-inch rule) in 2008. Since 1992, sawtimber volume increased 2.6 billion board feet or 68 percent. More than 47 percent of the volume increase was in 11.0 to 18.9 diameter classes totaling 1.2 billion board feet. All 2-inch diameter classes for sawtimber showed an increase of ≥25 percent except for the 33.0–34.9 diameter class.

Almost 81 percent (5.2 billion board feet) of the hardwood sawtimber volume was held by private landowners, with families or individuals holding 75 percent of all sawtimber volume (4.8 billion board feet). Since 1992, sawtimber volume increased almost 2.0 billion board feet on all private timberland and 575.0 million board feet on all public land.

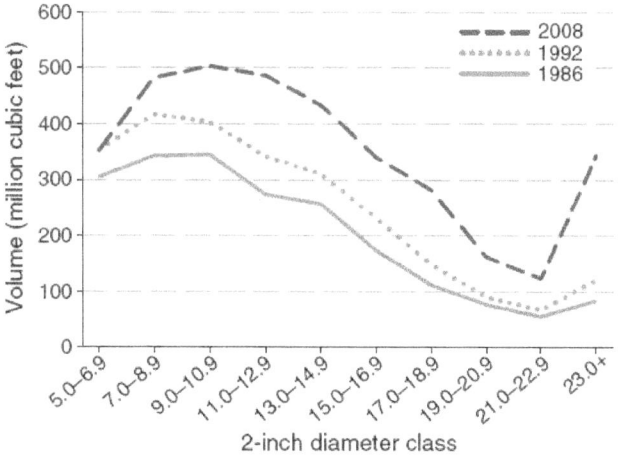

Figure 15—Merchantable volume of hardwood live trees on timberland by 2-inch diameter class and survey year, east Oklahoma.

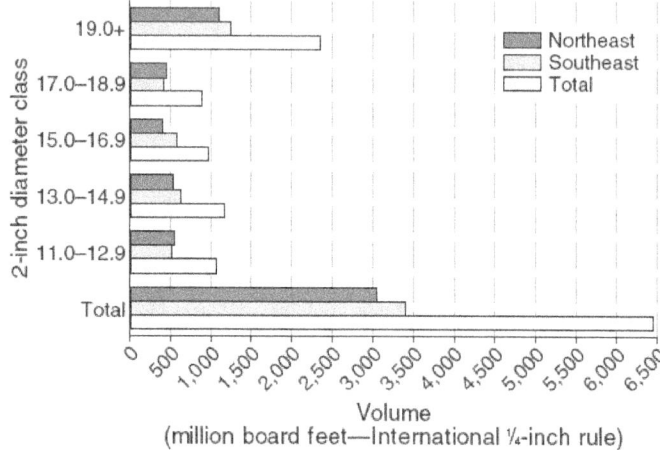

Figure 16—Hardwood sawtimber inventory volume on timberland by 2-inch diameter class and survey unit, east Oklahoma, 2008.

Components of Change

Net growth, removals, and mortality (GRM) comprise the components of change as reported by FIA. Current estimates of GRM are based on the remeasurement of previously forested plots (1992) that remained in a forested condition in the 2008 inventory cycle. However, the remeasurement occurred on the variable radius plots from the previous plot design and methodology. This was necessary because the new fixed radius plot design was established during the 2008 inventory.

Estimates of each component are expressed as the average annual value between the two inventories representing the years from 1993 to 2008. Average annual net growth is the total (or gross) growth minus mortality. Net growth and removals reflect the forest dynamics (natural and human induced) and were only slightly influenced by forest area change. When net growth exceeds removals, then net change is positive and inventory volume is increasing. The opposite is true when removals exceed net growth. These components of change help evaluate how much and why the forest inventory volume is changing. However, because net change is calculated from remeasured plots only, it does not account for all the change in volume between surveys. Of the 1,073 forested plots, 960 are remeasured plots in east Oklahoma.

Figure 17 shows the total average annual components of change of live-tree volume for the last two FIA surveys in east Oklahoma. While gross growth has increased for the 2008 survey, both mortality and removals have also increased since the 1992 inventory. However, net change remained positive in both inventory cycles, influencing total volume to reach an alltime high (fig. 10).

When assessing the impact of average annual net growth and removals, it is helpful to include total volume. Figure 18 places average annual net growth and

removals on the same scale with total live-tree volume for the survey period. Net change (net growth minus removals) equals 47 million cubic feet. This is a result of net growth outpacing removals by almost 37 percent. Comparing net change to total volume, the total inventory increased about 0.9 percent annually from 1993 to 2008. This average annual net increase is reflected in the increase of total inventory volume since the 1992 survey and represents a compounding increase of volume over the 16 years since the last inventory.

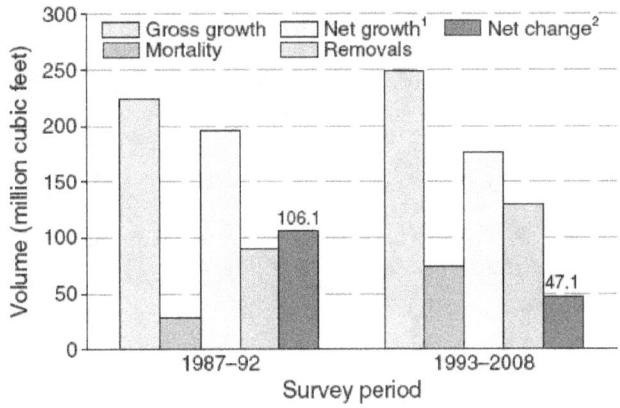

[1] Net growth = gross growth – mortality.
[2] Net change = net growth – removals.

Figure 17—Average annual components of change for live trees by survey period, east Oklahoma.

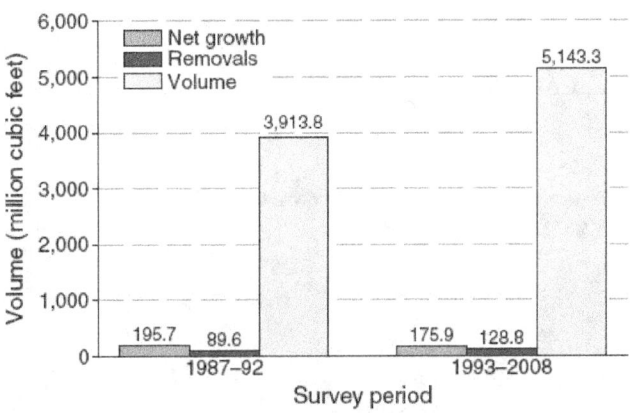

Figure 18—Average annual net growth and removals for live trees compared to total volume by survey period, east Oklahoma.

Softwood Average Annual Net Growth, Removals, and Mortality

In the discussion of volume, it was noted that softwood volume represented 32 percent of total inventory in 2008. However, the average annual growth of the softwood inventory represented 53 percent of the total average annual growth in east Oklahoma (softwood and hardwood). Softwood average annual net growth represented 5.7 percent of the softwood inventory and outpaced hardwood growth of the hardwood inventory by almost 2.5:1. Softwood net growth averaged 93.5 million cubic feet per year from 1993 to 2008 in east Oklahoma (fig. 19).

Softwood removals were 55 percent of all average annual removals in east Oklahoma during this survey period. Softwood removals represented 4.3 percent of the softwood inventory. Average annual softwood removals were 71.2 million cubic feet.

The average annual net growth showed a 17-percent decline from 112.0 million cubic feet in 1992 to 93.5 million cubic feet in 2008. For the same survey periods, removals have increased 27 percent from 56.0 million cubic feet (1992) to 71.2 million cubic feet (2008). Removals were still less than net growth (fig. 19).

Figure 20 shows the relationship of net growth and removals for softwoods and hardwoods expressed as a percent. Softwood net growth exceeded removals by 100 percent for the 1992 survey period. For the 2008 survey period net growth declined because of an increase in mortality and removals (fig. 19) which lowered the net change (fig. 17). However, net growth outpaced removals by 31 percent (fig. 20). This indicates that the total softwood inventory continued to increase and has been sustainable, but at a lesser rate than during the 1992 survey period.

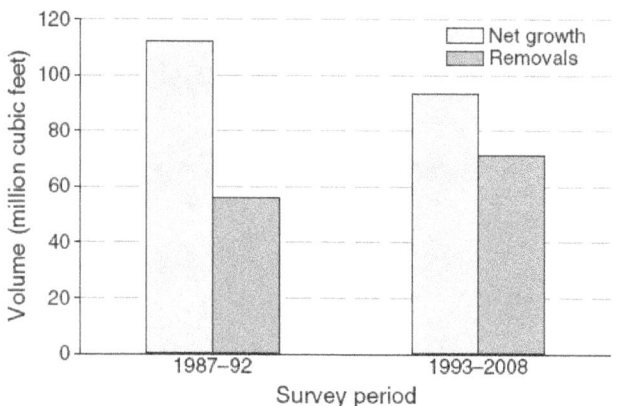

Figure 19—Average annual net growth and removals for softwood live trees by survey period, east Oklahoma.

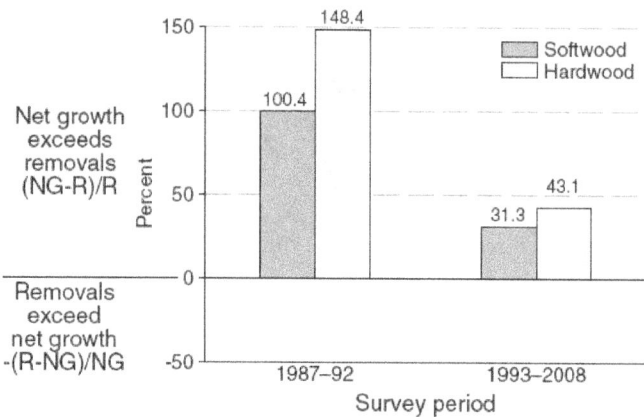

Figure 20—Percent increase or decrease relationship of average annual net growth and removals for live trees by survey period, east Oklahoma.

Thinning pine stands improves growth and health of the forest. (photo by Tony Johnson, Southern Research Station)

Softwood average annual mortality was 13.2 million cubic feet. When comparing tabular values, mortality increased 247 percent. Further investigation was necessary to determine if this was a reasonable change assessment for mortality.

It was determined that the 16 years between plot remeasurement represents an extended period for calculating net GRM. Average annual net growth and removals discussed above are comparable with historical survey values.

However, average annual mortality indicated a higher value than experienced in previous surveys. While the percent change appeared high, the total values were not excessive in relation to total inventory volume which increased 85 percent since 1976. Therefore, a comparison of mortality volume per acre showed current values 30 percent higher than in 1992, and 11 percent higher than in 1976.

Hardwood Average Annual Net Growth, Removals, and Mortality

Hardwood net growth averaged 82.4 million cubic feet per year during the remeasurement period from 1993 to 2008 in east Oklahoma. This was a 2-percent decline from 83.7 million cubic feet reported in 1992. The average annual growth of the hardwood inventory represented 47 percent of the total average annual growth (softwood and hardwood), and was about 2.4 percent of the hardwood inventory.

At 57.6 million cubic feet per year, average annual removals represented 45 percent of all removals and only 1.6 percent of the hardwood inventory. Although increasing by 71 percent (from 33.7 to 57.6 million cubic feet) removals were still less than net growth (fig. 21).

Similar to softwood, the hardwood net growth to removals relationship was still increasing the total hardwood inventory volume, but at a lesser rate than shown in the 1992 survey (fig. 20). Hardwood net growth exceeded removals 148 percent for the 1992 survey. For the 2008 survey period, net growth remained about the same as in 1992, but removals increased. Net growth outpaced removals by 43 percent.

Hardwood mortality also increased considerably. Average annual mortality was 60.2 million cubic feet in 2008, an increase of 146 percent (35.7 million cubic feet) since 1992. As with softwood mortality, the total values were not excessive in relation to total inventory volume (softwood and hardwood), which has increased 85 percent since 1976.

Harvest Removals, Timber Volume, and Sustainability

Since the 1960s, the forestry community in east Oklahoma has experienced and responded to many changes. Opportunities to expand existing forest products manufacturing facilities and locate new mills, including engineered forest products, have resulted in additional jobs for local economies and improved the quality of life. With socioeconomic development and demand for forest products, pressures on forest resources also offered opportunities for forest landowners to improve forest management on the landscape, as demonstrated by forest area, volume, and components of change comparisons (figs. 10 and 22).

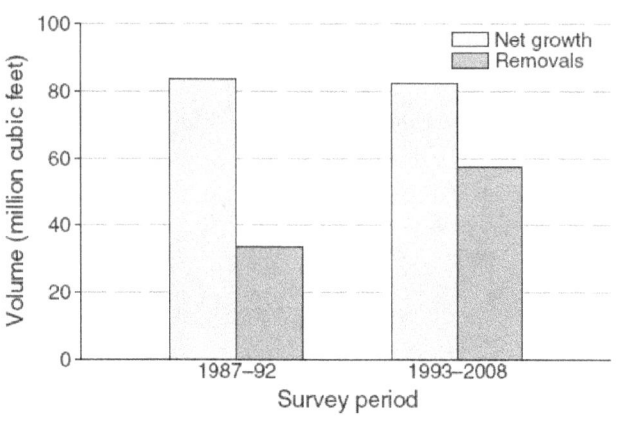

Figure 21—Average annual net growth and removals for hardwood live trees by survey period, east Oklahoma.

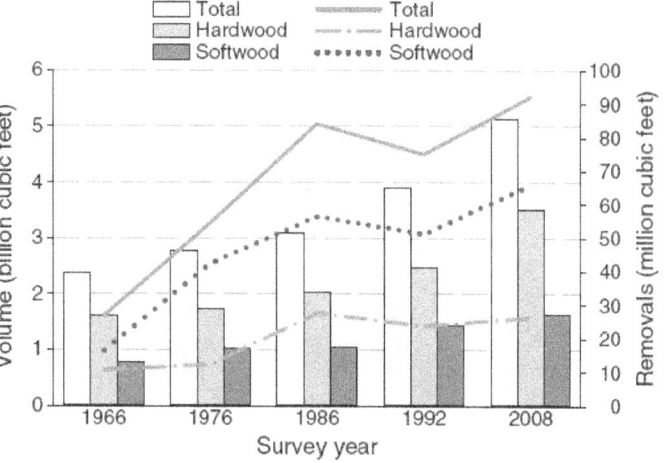

Figure 22—Comparison of inventory volume (live trees) to average annual removals (growing stock) by survey year, east Oklahoma.

For example, total average annual harvest removals of growing stock were at a historical high of 92.3 million cubic feet per year or 3.4 times 1966 levels (fig. 22). Despite this increase in harvest removals, volume more than doubled (increasing 117 percent).

Throughout most of the South, harvesting exerts more pressure on softwoods than hardwoods. Harvest removals of softwood growing stock represented 4 percent of the softwood volume in 2008, a quadrupling since 1966. Nevertheless, softwood live-tree volume more than doubled with an increase of 114 percent since 1966. Hardwood harvest removals

of growing stock represented <0.8 percent of the total hardwood live-tree volume. However, harvest removals have increased 147 percent since 1966 and volume has more than doubled.

Over the last 40 years, east Oklahoma has more than doubled total inventory volume of live trees for both softwood and hardwood despite a substantial increase for demand of forest products. While there are various definitions for forest sustainability, the increase in timber volume on a relatively stable land base certainly indicates a sustained yield over the long term, plus a substantial reserve for future generations.

Rock and forests near Daisy, Pushmataha County. (photo by Kurt Atkinson, Oklahoma Forestry Services)

Forest Disturbance

Timberland disturbance is part of the dynamics of a forest and can be separated into two categories: 1) planned forest management treatments and 2) forest disturbances, both of which are expressed as average annual area or volume estimates. Forest treatments are part of the forest operations management tools or silvicultural methods such as various harvesting systems, site preparation, tree planting, prescribed burning, or natural regeneration. Forest disturbances include insect and disease outbreaks, wildfires, weather events, animal, grazing, and human activities such as land clearing.

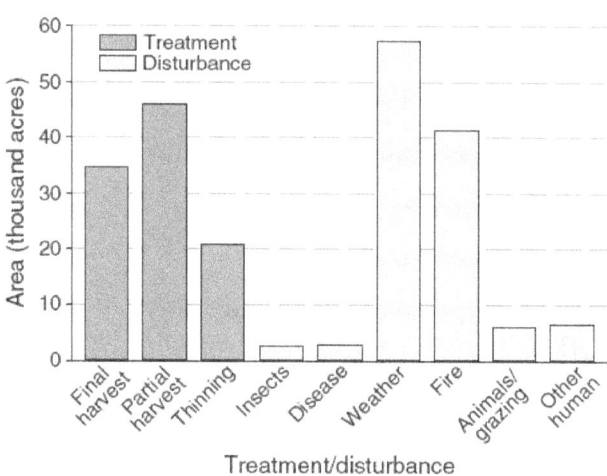

Figure 23—Average area treated/disturbed annually by treatment and disturbance types, east Oklahoma, 2008.

Forest Management Treatments

Some form of harvesting or timber stand improvement occurred on 101,900 acres annually during the survey period from 1993 to 2008. This represents 2 percent of the total timberland area each year. Final harvests averaged 34,500 acres each year during this survey or 0.7 percent of all timberland area (fig. 23). About 45,100 acres experienced a partial harvest and 21,000 acres were thinned. Combined,

these two harvest operations represented about 1.3 percent of all timberland. About 400 acres a year received some type of other stand improvement.

Tree planting and direct seeding occurred on 22,500 acres each year, compared to 12,200 acres that were regenerated naturally. The combined forest regeneration represented about 0.7 percent of the total timberland area each year.

Prescribed fire is an important tool for timber management and wildlife habitat. (photo courtesy of Oklahoma Forestry Services)

Natural Disturbances

Most disturbances are natural occurrences and have greatly contributed to forest dynamics throughout history. Quite often, disturbances affect small areas and contribute to species richness. However, some large-scale disturbances—such as intense fires, epidemic insect and disease outbreaks, and major weather events—can be catastrophic.

The largest area of damage resulted from weather events, specifically ice storms (80 percent). The average annual damage from weather was 57,300 acres occurring mostly in the oak-hickory forest type. Fire, which plays a major influence on plant ecology over time, experienced about 41,300 acres damage as an average annual occurrence. Fire damage includes both wild-fire and prescribed burning.

Damage from other disturbance agents totaled about 17,900 acres annually: beavers and domestic grazing (6,100 acres), land clearing and other human activities (6,400 acres), diseases (2,900 acres), and insects (2,500 acres).

Note: The average annual treated or disturbed areas discussed are based on the forest-type group that was present at the end of the previous survey. Tables published on the FIA Web site were based on the current forest-type group (that was present at the time of the remeasurement). Depending on user goals, there are benefits to both types of presentation of these types of data, but data based upon the forest condition of the previous measurement has the most utility for general users.

Natural disturbances, such as ice storms, contribute to mortality and damaged timber may be salvaged in a quick harvest operation. (photo by Craig Marquardt, Oklahoma Forestry Services)

Timber Removals, Utilization, and Residues

Introduction

In addition to collecting plot data, FIA canvasses primary forest product mills every 2 to 3 years regarding delivered roundwood logs, pulpwood, and chips hauled directly from timberland and conducts logging utilization studies. These data are integrated with FIA plot data to assess wood product flow and production.

This section relates to and expands the discussion of removals discussed in the components of change section regarding roundwood logs harvested and delivered to primary wood product mills such as saw-mills, veneer mills, pole mills, pulpwood chip mills, oriented strand board mill, and other wood processing facilities using logs and chips.

With emerging bioenergy markets appearing throughout the South, this section also addresses logging residues and the potential availability and recovery.

Timber Removals and Utilization

Average annual timber removals include the merchantable and nonmerchantable volume of trees harvested for products and whole trees or portions of trees cut and left behind as logging residue. Average annual removals volume also includes trees removed due to land clearing for agriculture or urban development and timberland set aside by statute prohibiting tree harvesting. The latter removals are considered land use change removals. Total removals include harvested products, logging residues, and land use removals and are usually reported by broad species group at the regional, State, FIA survey unit, or county level for ownership, forest type, diameter class, and other variables.

Most FIA removal tables report only the merchantable portion or volume from a 1-foot stump to the 4-inch top in cubic feet for trees ≥5 inches d.b.h. For sawtimber size trees, removals are reported in board feet (International ¼-inch rule), as well. Removal estimates are generated for the sawtimber portion, growing-stock trees, and all-live trees which include rough and rotten cull trees. It is best to think of these categories for removals as subsets; sawtimber removals are a subset of growing-stock removals, growing-stock removals are a subset of all-live tree removals, and all of these are a subset of total aboveground tree removals which include the volume of the stumps, tops, and limbs to 1-inch in diameter. Volume of removal trees <5 inches d.b.h. have been considered noncommercial and have not been reported on a routine basis.

Reporting removals in this fashion served FIA and its users well for many decades when dealing with the traditional timber products such as saw logs, veneer logs, poles, and other solid-wood forest products. However, the traditional fiber products industries (pulpwood, composite panel, and mulch) along with the emerging bioenergy industry have and will dramatically increase the utilization of rough and cull trees, tops and limbs, a portion of trees <5 inches d.b.h., and in some cases, understory vegetation.

The majority of timber bought and sold commercially has been scaled by weight at the destination mills for many years. The forestry community has become familiar with weight as a unit of measure for timber products and has requested FIA to include weight as a reporting unit for removals volumes. The cubic foot volumes have been converted to green tons throughout this section using 69.36 pounds per cubic foot for softwoods and 80.10 pounds per cubic foot for hardwoods.[4] It is important to

---

[4] Bentley, James W. 2011. [Untitled]. [Unpaged]. Unpublished data. On file with: Southern Research Station, Forest Inventory and Analysis, 4700 Old Kingston Pike, Knoxville, TN 37919.

Improvements in harvesting machines cut most trees near ground level and increases utilization. (photos by Tony Johnson, Southern Research Station)

keep in mind that this is fresh green weight of wood and bark per cubic foot of wood immediately after harvest.

This section focuses on total average annual removals for all-live tree volume for trees ≥ 5 inches d.b.h. expressed in cubic feet of solid wood and green tons of wood and bark. It also includes an estimate of removals of wood volume in cubic feet, and wood and bark weight in green tons for stumps, tops, and limbs and expressed as average annual harvest removals from nonmerchantable sources. In addition, an estimate of removals for trees < 5 inches d.b.h. is discussed under the section for logging residue and is not included in total annual removals. Figure 24 shows the total annual removals by the subcategories previously discussed.

Between 1993 and 2008, total removals from all sources in east Oklahoma, for both softwoods and hardwoods totaled 161.4 million cubic feet, or 6.0 million tons (tables 3 and 4). Softwoods accounted for 55 percent of total removals, 88.2 million cubic feet (3.1 million green tons). Volume of removals attributed to the merchantable portion of all-live tree removals accounted for 128.8 million cubic feet (4.8 million green tons), while nonmerchantable sources accounted for 32.6 million cubic feet (1.2 million green tons).

The following sections present the average annual estimates for the merchantable and nonmerchantable portions of annual roundwood product output (roundwood delivered to mills), land use removals, and estimates of logging residue, in east Oklahoma.

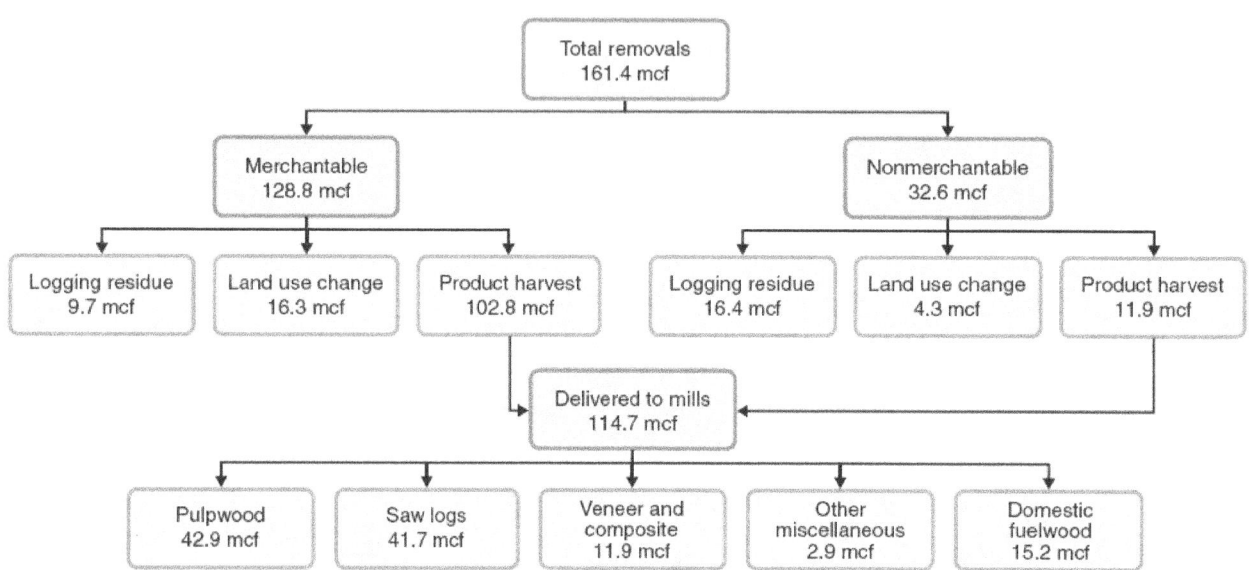

Figure 24—Total harvest merchandizing from the forest to mills by merchantability class and product category, east Oklahoma, 2008 (mcf = million cubic feet).

Table 3—Average annual volume of all-live timber removals by removals class, species group, and source, east Oklahoma from 1993 to 2008

Removals class and species group	All sources	Source[a]	
		Merchantable	Non-merchantable
		thousand cubic feet	
Roundwood products			
Softwood	74,406	64,528	9,878
Hardwood	40,273	38,259	2,014
Total	114,679	102,787	11,892
Logging residues			
Softwood	10,079	3,705	6,374
Hardwood	16,037	6,030	10,007
Total	26,116	9,735	16,381
Land use removals			
Softwood	3,724	3,008	716
Hardwood	16,923	13,310	3,613
Total	20,647	16,318	4,329
Total removals			
Softwood	88,209	71,241	16,968
Hardwood	73,233	57,599	15,634
Total	161,442	128,840	32,602

Numbers in rows and columns may not sum to totals due to rounding.
[a] All-live removals.

Table 4—Average annual green weight of timber removals by removals class, species group, and source, east Oklahoma from 1993 to 2008

Removals class and species group	All sources	Source[a] Merchantable	Non-merchantable
		green tons	
Roundwood products			
Softwood	2,580,636	2,238,028	342,608
Hardwood	1,612,869	1,532,213	80,656
Total	4,193,505	3,770,241	423,264
Logging residues			
Softwood	349,577	128,501	221,076
Hardwood	642,249	241,492	400,757
Total	991,826	369,993	621,833
Land use removals			
Softwood	129,161	104,327	24,834
Hardwood	677,737	533,045	144,692
Total	806,898	637,372	169,526
Total removals			
Softwood	3,059,374	2,470,856	588,518
Hardwood	2,932,855	2,306,750	626,105
Total	5,992,229	4,777,606	1,214,623

Numbers in rows and columns may not sum to totals due to rounding.
[a] All-live removals.

Timber Products

Estimates of timber product output (TPO) and mill residues were obtained from canvasses (questionnaires) sent to all major primary wood-using mills in east Oklahoma. The canvasses were used to determine the types and amount of roundwood (i.e., saw logs, pulpwood, plywood and veneer, poles, etc.) received by each mill, the county of origin, the species used, and how the mills disposed of the bark and wood residues produced. The canvasses were conducted every 3 years by personnel from the Southern Research Station and Oklahoma Forestry Services. These data were used to augment the FIA annual inventory of all-live timber removals by providing the proportions that are used for timber products. Individual TPO studies, or industry surveys, are necessary to track

A load of logs from McCurtain County. (photo by Al Myatt, Oklahoma Forestry Services)

29

trends and capture changes in product output levels. Industry surveys conducted in 1996, 1999, 2002, and 2005 were used to determine average annual product output for roundwood and plant byproducts for the latest FIA cycle (Howell and Johnson 1998, Howell and Johnson 2002, Johnson and others 2005, Johnson and others 2008). This means that the average volumes reported in this section for individual products will not match specific year values reported in TPO publications or online query tools.

Volume utilized or delivered for roundwood products totaled 114.7 million cubic feet (4.2 million green tons), or 71 percent of total removals. Nonmerchantable sources from all-live removals accounted for 11.9 million cubic feet (423,300 green tons), or 10 percent of roundwood product output levels. Average annual output of softwood roundwood products (including domestic fuelwood) totaled 74.4 million cubic feet

(2.6 million green tons) and accounted for 65 percent of the total roundwood product output. Average annual hardwood output totaled 40.3 million cubic feet (1.6 million green tons).

As shown in tables 5 and 6, pulpwood was the leading product, accounting for 38 percent of total product output. Average annual output for pulpwood roundwood (softwood and hardwood combined) totaled 42.9 million cubic feet (1.6 million green tons). Combined output of saw logs averaged 41.7 million cubic feet (1.5 million green tons) and accounted for 36 percent of total product output. Volume used for domestic fuelwood totaled 15.2 million cubic feet (607,000 green tons) and accounted for 13 percent of total product output. Veneer and composite panel production combined totaled 11.9 million cubic feet (413,000 green tons), or 10 percent of total output.

Table 5—Average annual timber removals from all sources on timberland by product, softwood, and hardwood, east Oklahoma from 1993 to 2008

Product	All species	Softwood	Hardwood
	thousand cubic feet		
Roundwood products			
Saw logs	41,705	34,190	7,515
Veneer logs and bolts	10,323	10,288	35
Pulpwood	42,937	25,157	17,780
Composite panels	1,578	1,578	0
Other	2,934	2,934	0
Residential fuelwood	15,202	259	14,943
All products	114,679	74,406	40,273
Logging residues	26,116	10,079	16,037
Land use removals	20,647	3,724	16,923
Total removals	161,442	88,209	73,233

Table 6—Average annual timber removals from all sources on timberland by product, softwood, and hardwood, east Oklahoma from 1993 to 2008

Product	All species	Softwood	Hardwood
	green tons		
Roundwood products			
Saw logs	1,486,793	1,185,817	300,976
Veneer logs and bolts	358,223	356,821	1,402
Pulpwood	1,584,614	872,525	712,089
Composite panels	54,730	54,730	0
Other	101,760	101,760	0
Residential fuelwood	607,385	8,983	598,402
All products	4,193,505	2,580,636	1,612,869
Logging residues	991,826	349,577	642,249
Land use removals	806,898	129,161	677,737
Total removals	5,992,229	3,059,374	2,932,855

Log separation for product merchandizing. (photo by Tony Johnson, Southern Research Station)

Mill Residue

Mill residues are defined as wood material generated in the production of timber products from roundwood at primary manufacturing facilities. This material falls into three main categories:

• Coarse residues, or material, such as slabs, edgings, trim, veneer cores and ends, which are suitable for chipping,

• Fine residues, or material, such as sawdust, shavings, and veneer residue, which are not suitable for chipping, and

• Bark which is used mainly for industrial fuel.

For many years, most mill residue produced in east Oklahoma has been utilized either for primary products such as pulp or in secondary products such as mulch and animal bedding, or as fuel at wood product mills.

Table 7 shows the average annual disposal and utilization of mill residue. Data regarding mill residue production

Logs stacked high at the Huber OSB plant at Broken Bow. (photo by Kurt Atkinson, Oklahoma Forestry Services)

Table 7—Average annual disposal of residue at primary wood-using plants by product, species group, and type of residue, east Oklahoma from 1993 to 2008

Product and species group	All types	Type of residue			
		Bark	Coarse	Sawdust	Shavings
		thousand cubic feet			
Fiber products					
Softwood	13,604	0	13,604	0	0
Hardwood	1,383	0	1,383	0	0
Total	14,987	0	14,987	0	0
Particleboard					
Softwood	709	0	379	0	330
Hardwood	0	0	0	0	0
Total	709	0	379	0	330
Charcoal/ chemical wood					
Softwood	10	0	10	0	0
Hardwood	0	0	0	0	0
Total	10	0	10	0	0
Sawn products					
Softwood	3,644	0	3,644	0	0
Hardwood	2	0	2	0	0
Total	3,646	0	3,646	0	0
Industrial fuel					
Softwood	21,686	8,472	255	10,556	2,402
Hardwood	4,184	1,814	1,007	1,364	0
Total	25,870	10,286	1,262	11,920	2,402
Miscellaneous					
Softwood	2,983	1,045	4	1	1,935
Hardwood	977	162	317	468	31
Total	3,960	1,206	320	468	1,966
Not used					
Softwood	2	0	1	1	0
Hardwood	18	3	10	6	0
Total	20	3	11	6	0
All products					
Softwood	42,637	9,517	17,896	10,557	4,667
Hardwood	6,564	1,978	2,717	1,837	31
Total	49,200	11,495	20,613	12,395	4,697

Numbers in rows and columns may not sum to totals due to rounding.

and disposal was generated by averaging TPO forest industry survey years representing the FIA survey time period and indicated that 49 million cubic feet of wood and bark residue was generated from primary processors. Sawmills and veneer mills generated the majority of the mill residue produced. Bark accounted for 11.5 million cubic feet (23 percent), coarse residues accounted for 20.6 million cubic feet (42 percent), and sawdust and shavings accounted for 17.1 million cubic feet (35 percent) of mill residue produced.

With nearly 53 percent (25.9 million cubic feet) used for industrial fuel, either at pulpmills for boiler fuel or at sawmills for dry kiln operations, industrial fuel was the largest use of mill residue. Bark at 10.3 million cubic feet and sawdust at 11.9 million cubic feet together accounted for 86 percent of mill residue used for fuel. Eighty-nine percent of the bark residue was used for fuel, with the remainder going for mulch or miscellaneous products. Seventy-three percent of the coarse residue, 15.0 million tons, was used for pulp or fiber products.

Land Use Removals

Tables 3 and 4 show that land use removals (land clearing or reserved forest land) or removal volume attributed to land use change accounted for 13 percent of total removals (20.6 million cubic feet or 807,000 green tons). The merchantable portion of live trees accounted for 16.3 million cubic feet (637,000 green tons), compared to 4.3 million cubic feet (170,000 green tons) for nonmerchantable sources.

Logging Residue

The merchantable portions of trees cut and left onsite are underutilized removals by FIA merchantability standards, while the nonmerchantable portions of trees (part of the 1-foot stump or volume in tops <4 inches d.b.h.) used for products are considered overutilized removals by FIA merchantability standards. With this in mind, under- and over-utilization factors used to determine average annual logging residue estimates used in this section were derived from the 2008 east Oklahoma harvest and utilization study (see footnote 4 on p. 26). Logging residue, which traditionally had little marketable value, has been considered a possible source for bioenergy and other timber products during recent years. It is important to keep in mind that logging residue, traditionally, has had little marketable value. Retrieval of logging residue is a matter of economics and markets. If markets are available and consumers are willing to pay a reasonable price, then more total tree volume (including what has been left as logging residues) may be used for products.

Most loggers are setup to merchandise the main bole of the tree or the merchantable portion of trees (from a 1-foot stump to a 4-inch top d.b.h.). The current conventional logging system in east Oklahoma consists of a feller buncher, one or two rubber-tired grapple skidders, a delimbing gate or pull-through delimber at the deck, a knuckleboom loader, and tractor-trailers to haul the volume harvested. Improved mechanization and equipment capabilities have dramatically increased productivity and utilization across the South. These systems are typically capable of producing on average about 10 loads per day of tree-length wood.[5]

Overlook of the expanse of forest in east Oklahoma. (photo by Linda Doss, Oklahoma Forestry Services)

Woody material typically left on a logging site includes:

1. Whole trees, ≥ 5 inches d.b.h., or portions of the merchantable boles of trees severed and broken and left during the felling operation (merchantable logging residues),

2. Small trees, <5 inches d.b.h., damaged or killed during harvesting operations (nonmerchantable logging residues), and

3. Residual stump portions, tops, and limbs or forks not utilized because of insufficient size or quality to fit on the trailers (nonmerchantable logging residues).

This wood material is known as merchantable and nonmerchantable logging residues.

The merchantable portion of logging residue was calculated in a two-stage process. First, for those plots that were classified as

---

[5] Personal communication. 2008. H.M. (Mac) Lupold, Lupold Consulting, Inc., 224 Chestnut Ferry Road, Camden, SC 29020.

timberland during both the previous and current inventories, field crews identified the volume of whole trees cut and not utilized during remeasurement. A removal volume was derived for trees that were classified in this category.

Second, underutilization factors derived from felled-tree utilization studies were applied to the volume classified as utilized by field crews for the remainder of the merchantable portion of logging residue. For example, felled-tree utilization studies conducted for east Oklahoma showed that only 4 percent of the merchantable softwood bole was not utilized for products, while 11 percent of the merchantable hardwood bole was not utilized. Please keep in mind that total removal volume consists of volume from the merchantable and nonmerchantable portions of removal trees. Overutilization factors from the utilization studies were used to determine how much of the nonmerchantable portion of removals was used for timber products. The nonmerchantable volume was calculated for the land use change removal estimate and added to the merchantable volume for a total land use change removal volume. The volume of nonmerchantable logging residues was calculated by subtracting the nonmerchantable portion of timber products and land use change values from total volume of nonmerchantable removals.

Based on these calculations and the data in tables 3, 4, 5, and 6, the annual logging residue volume in east Oklahoma from 1993 to 2008 averaged 26.1 million cubic feet per year, or 992,000 green tons, or 16 percent of total timber removals. Nearly 10.1 million cubic feet (350,000 green tons), or 39 percent of the logging residues generated came from softwoods, while 16.0 million cubic feet (642,000 green tons) came from hardwoods. Logging residue from the merchantable portion of

all-live tree removals totaled 9.7 million cubic feet per year (370,000 green tons), or >37 percent of total logging residue. It is interesting to note that while total logging residue accounted for 16 percent of total removals, the merchantable portion of logging residue for both softwood and hardwood combined accounted for about 8 percent of total live removals. For softwoods, the merchantable portion of logging residue accounted for 5 percent of the total softwood all-live tree removals (71.2 million cubic feet). The merchantable portion of hardwood logging residue accounted for 10 percent of total all-live hardwood removals (57.6 million cubic feet). Nonmerchantable sources (such as the residual stump, forks, and tops and limbs) accounted for 16.4 million cubic feet (622,000 green tons), or 63 percent of total logging residue. Trees <5 inches d.b.h. contributed another 513,000 green tons of possible logging residue.

Over the same time period, the area of timber harvested annually in east Oklahoma was 101,900 acres: 34,500 acres (34 percent) in final harvests, 45,100 acres (44 percent) in partial harvests, and 21,000 acres (21 percent) in commercial thinning operations. The removals volume attributed to timber products and logging residues relate directly to these treated acres. Based on these estimates, nearly 51 tons per acre in the merchantable and nonmerchantable portion of trees ≥5 inches d.b.h. were removed annually. Of this, >41 tons per acre were utilized for products, while 9.7 tons per acre were left as logging residue after discounting the residual stump volume. Adding in 5.0 tons per acre for trees <5 inches d.b.h., the total logging residue amounted to 14.7 tons per acre. This volume would be the equivalent of about one-half a tree-length trailer load of wood for every acre treated in east Oklahoma.

Utilization of logging residues. (photo by Tony Johnson, Southern Research Station)

Potential Recoverable Logging Residue

Conventional logging operations are designed to haul tree length wood that is securely placed between the stanchions of the trailer for hauling. A more effective way to handle the nonmerchantable portion of removals trees—rough trees with crooked boles, tops, and limbs—is to chip this material at the site and transport it in chip vans. Some east Oklahoma loggers have begun to add whole-tree chippers and chip vans to their inventory of equipment. Current markets for chipped wood captured from logging residue are limited to facilities with wood fired boiler systems or production of mulch. Where bioenergy or mulch markets are available, onsite chipping is a cost efficient way of handling and transporting rough and rotten trees, the nonmerchantable portions of cut trees, and small trees < 5 inches d.b.h.

What is a realistic recovery rate of logging residue in east Oklahoma? Current literature and personal communications with loggers and others in the forestry field suggest that conventional logging operations described above could capture about 60 percent of the material currently left behind as logging residue. This recovery rate excludes residual stump volume and would seem to be a realistic goal for possible extraction of unused material (Perlack and others 2005).

For this assessment, the total non-merchantable portion of logging residue has been reduced by 64 percent to 222,000 green tons to account for residual stump (132,000 green tons) and tops and limb volume (269,000 green tons) that are not immediately recoverable (table 8). This amount combined with the merchantable logging residue of 259,000 green tons leaves a total of 481,000 green tons available from trees ≥ 5 inches d.b.h., or 4.7 tons per acre. Residual volume following harvest operations for trees < 5 inches d.b.h. account for another 513,000 green tons. This report assumes only 20 percent could realistically be extracted, or almost 103,000 green tons for an additional 1.0 ton per acre (see footnote 5 on page 33). Combined, the average annual recovery of logging residue at a 60-percent recovery rate from all sources could have amounted to an additional 5.7 tons per acre added to the product stream.

35

Table 8—Average annual volume of logging residue by size class, recovery potential, east Oklahoma from 1993 to 2008

Logging residue in harvested trees by size class	Total		Non-recoverable		Total available		Potentially recoverable at 60% recovery rate[a]		
			Discounted stump volume	Discounted <5" volume	Base total volume	Total	Discounted >5" volume	Total volume	Total
	green tons	tons/ acre	--------- green tons ---------			tons/ acre	---- green tons ----		tons/ acre
Merchantable volume >5"	369,993	3.6	0	0	369,993	3.6	110,998	258,995	2.5
Nonmerchantable volume >5"	621,833	6.1	131,551	0	490,332	4.9	268,518	221,814	2.2
Total	991,826	9.7	131,551	0	860,325	8.5	379,516	480,809	4.7
Nonmerchantable volume <5"	513,118	5.0	0	410,494	102,624	1.0	0	102,624	1.0
All classes	1,504,944	14.7	131,551	410,494	962,949	9.5	379,516	583,433	5.7

Numbers in rows and columns may not sum to totals due to rounding.
[a] This value is calculated from the base total volume of 962,949 tons.

Summary—Outlook for Underutilized Material

Traditional markets for paper and construction materials remain the dominant wood products industry. However, timber removals and utilization continue to change as increased demand for wood as a source for energy create new market opportunities.

FIA inventory and TPO survey data indicate that a substantial amount of fiber is currently underutilized and could be used for bioenergy or other timber products if effectively captured. Future development of facilities that utilize wood for energy may provide opportunities to capture logging residue and minimize future increases to harvest levels. This will require further study.

New markets, such as bioenergy facilities that plan to use logging residues as a primary source for fuel, must carefully assess average annual volume available in a procurement area, and consider incentives to attract loggers to invest in operations that harvest wood residues at minimum costs.

With proper assessment, investment, and operation, industries utilizing logging residues could offer opportunities for a renewable energy source while creating "green" jobs. Loggers could realize additional markets for fiber and additional sources of income from each logging site. And landowners could earn additional income with increased utilization from harvested acres and, at the same time, lower site preparation costs when establishing new forests.

Bechtold, W.A.; Patterson, P.L., Editors. 2005. The enhanced forest inventory and analysis program—national sampling design and estimation procedures. Gen. Tech. Rep. SRS–80. Asheville, NC: U.S. Department of Agriculture Forest Service, Southern Research Station. 85 p.

Beers, T.W.; Miller, C.I. 1964. Point sampling: research results, theory and applications. Resour. Bull. 786. Lafayette, IN: Purdue University Agricultural Experiment Station. 55 p.

Earles, J.M. 1976. Forest statistics for east Oklahoma counties. Resour. Bull. SO–62. New Orleans: U.S. Department of Agriculture Forest Service, Southern Forest Experiment Station. 40 p.

Eldredge, I.F.; Cruikshank, J.W. 1938. Forest resources of southeast Oklahoma. For. Surv. Rel. 37. New Orleans: U.S. Department of Agriculture Forest Service, Southern Forest Experiment Station. 25 p.

Canoeing is one of the many benefits of well-managed timberland. (photo courtesy of Oklahoma Forestry Services)

Fenneman, N.M. 1938. Physiography of Eastern United States. New York: McGraw-Hill. 714 p. [plus maps].

Harper, R.A.; McClure, N.D.; Johnson, T.G. [and others]. 2009. Georgia's forests, 2004. Resour. Bull. SRS–149. Asheville, NC: U.S. Department of Agriculture Forest Service, Southern Research Station. 78 p.

Hines, F.D.; Bertelson, D.F. 1987. Forest statistics for east Oklahoma counties, 1986. Resour. Bull. SO–121. New Orleans: U.S. Department of Agriculture Forest Service, Southern Forest Experiment Station. 57 p.

Howell, M.; Johnson, T.G. 1998. Oklahoma's timber industry—an assessment of timber product output and use, 1996. Resour. Bull. SRS–30. Asheville, NC: U.S. Department of Agriculture Forest Service, Southern Research Station. 16 p.

Howell, M.; Johnson, T.G. 2002. Oklahoma's timber industry—an assessment of timber product output and use, 1999. Resour. Bull. SRS–82. Asheville, NC: U.S. Department of Agriculture Forest Service, Southern Research Station. 28 p.

Johnson, T.G.; Howell, M.; Bentley, J.W. 2005. Oklahoma's timber industry—an assessment of timber product output and use, 2002. Resour. Bull. SRS–100. Asheville, NC: U.S. Department of Agriculture Forest Service, Southern Research Station. 34 p.

Johnson, T.G.; Howell, M.; Bentley, J.W. 2008. Oklahoma's timber industry—an assessment of timber product output and use, 2005. Resour. Bull. SRS–136. Asheville, NC: U.S. Department of Agriculture Forest Service, Southern Research Station. 28 p.

Little, E.L., Jr. 1979. Checklist of United States trees (native and naturalized). Agric. Handb. 541. Washington, DC: U.S. Department of Agriculture. 375 p.

McClure, J.P.; Knight, H.A. 1984. Empirical yields of timber and forest biomass in the southeast. Res. Pap. SE–245. Asheville, NC: U.S. Department of Agriculture Forest Service, Southeastern Forest Experiment Station. 75 p.

McClure, J.P.; Saucier, J.R.; Biesterfeldt, R.C. 1981. Biomass in southeastern forests. Res. Pap. SE–227. Asheville, NC: U.S. Department of Agriculture Forest Service, Southeastern Forest Experiment Station. 38 p.

Miles, P.D. 2010. Forest inventory EVALIDator web-application version 4.01 beta. St. Paul, MN: U.S. Department of Agriculture Forest Service, Northern Research Station. http://apps.fs.fed.us/Evalidator/tmattribute.jsp.

Perlack, R.D.; Wright, L.L.; Turhollow, A. [and others]. 2005. Biomass as feedstock for a bioenergy and bioproducts industry: the technical feasibility of a billion-ton annual supply. Washington, DC: U.S. Department of Energy and U.S. Department of Agriculture Forest Service. ORNL/TM-2005/66. 73 p.

Rohlf, F.J.; Sokal, R.R. 1969. Statistical tables. San Francisco: W.H. Freeman and Company. 253 p.

Rosson, J.F., Jr. 1995. The timberland and woodland resources of central and west Oklahoma, 1989. Resour. Bull. SO–193. New Orleans: U.S. Department of Agriculture Forest Service, Southern Forest Experiment Station. 35 p.

Rosson, J.F., Jr. 2001. Forest resources of east Oklahoma, 1993. Resour. Bull. SRS–58, Asheville, NC: U.S. Department of Agriculture Forest Service, Southern Research Station. 75 p.

Rosson, J.F., Jr.; Rose, A.K. 2010. Arkansas' forests, 2005. Resour. Bull. SRS–166. Asheville, NC: U.S. Department of Agriculture Forest Service, Southern Research Station. 126 p.

Sternitzke, H.S.; Van Sickle, C.C. 1968. East Oklahoma forests. Resour. Bull. SO–14. New Orleans: U.S. Department of Agriculture Forest Service, Southern Forest Experiment Station. 32 p.

U.S. Department of Agriculture Forest Service. 1992. Forest resource inventories: an overview. Washington, DC: U.S. Department of Agriculture Forest Service, Forest Inventory, Economics, and Recreation Research. 39 p.

U.S. Department of Agriculture Forest Service. 2004a. Forest inventory and analysis national core field guide: field data collection procedures for phase 2 plots. Version 2.0. Washington, DC. 208 p. Vol. I. Internal report. On file with: U.S. Department of Agriculture Forest Service, Forest Inventory and Analysis, 201 14th Street, Washington, DC 20250.

U.S. Department of Agriculture Forest Service. 2004b. Forest inventory and analysis national core field guide: field data collection procedures for phase 3 plots. Version 2.0. Washington, DC. 164 p. Vol. II. Internal report. On file with: U.S. Department of Agriculture Forest Service, Forest Inventory and Analysis, 201 14th Street, Washington, DC 20250.

U.S. Department of Agriculture Natural Resources Conservation Service. 2006. The PLANTS database. Baton Rouge, LA: National Plant Data Center. http://plants. usda.gov. [Date accessed: October 17, 2011].

Van Duesen, P.C.; Dell, T.R.; Thomas, C.E. 1986. Volume growth estimation from permanent horizontal points. Forest Science. 32(2): 415–422.

Vigil, J.F.; Pike, R.J.; Howell, D.G. 2000. A tapestry of time and terrain: U.S. Geological Survey Geologic Investigations Series 2720. 1 plate scale 1:2,500,000, http://tapestry.usgs.gov/Default.html. [Date accessed: October 17, 2011]. 1 pamphlet, http://pubs.usgs.gov/imap/ i2720/ [Date accessed: October 17, 2011].

Afforestation—Area of land previously classified as nonforest that is converted to forest by planting trees or by natural reversion to forest.

All-live biomass—Weight of trees which includes all trees ≥1.0 inches d.b.h. See biomass.

All-live trees—All living trees ≥1.0 inch in d.b.h. All tree sizes, tree classes, and both commercial and noncommercial species are included. Note: live trees include all living trees ≥5.0 inches in d.b.h. Also, see definitions for live trees, live-tree volume, and all-live biomass.

All-live tree volume—Cubic-foot volume of all living trees ≥1.0 inch in d.b.h. All tree classes, and both commercial and noncommercial species are included. Also, see definitions for live trees, live-tree volume, and all-live biomass.

Average annual mortality—Average annual volume of trees ≥5.0 inches d.b.h. that died during the intersurvey period.

Average annual removals—Average annual volume of trees ≥5.0 inches d.b.h. removed from the inventory by harvesting, cultural operations (such as timber-stand improvement), land clearing, or changes in land use during the intersurvey period.

Average net annual growth—Average annual net change in volume of trees ≥5.0 inches d.b.h. (gross growth minus mortality) during the intersurvey period.

Basal area—The area in square feet of the cross section at breast height of a single tree or of all the trees in a stand, usually expressed in square feet per acre.

Biomass—The aboveground oven-dry weight of solid wood and bark in live trees ≥1.0-inch d.b.h., from ground level to the tip of the tree.

Blind check—A reinstallation of a field measurement plot done by a qualified inspection crew without production crew data on hand for the purpose of obtaining a measure of data quality. All plot-level information, and at least two subplots are fully remeasured.

Bole—That portion of a tree between a 1-foot stump and a 4-inch top d.o.b. in trees ≥5.0 inches d.b.h. Also called the merchantable bole or merchantable stem.

Carbon (weight)—For the core tables, the weight of carbon in wood is derived by multiplying oven-dry weight of wood (biomass) by 0.5. See biomass definition.

Census water—Streams, sloughs, estuaries, canals, and other moving bodies of water ≥200-feet wide, and lakes, reservoirs, ponds, and other permanent bodies of water ≥4.5 acres in area.

Cold check—An inspection done either as part of the training process, or as part of the ongoing Quality Control (QC) program. Normally the installation crew is not present at the time of inspection and the inspector has the completed data in-hand at the time of inspection. This type of quality control measurement is a "blind" measurement in that the crews do not know when or which of their plots will be remeasured by the inspection crew and cannot therefore alter their performance because of knowledge that the plot is a QA plot.

Commercial species—Tree species currently or potentially suitable for industrial wood products.

Compacted area—Type of compaction measured as part of the soil indicator. Examples include the junction areas of skid trails, landing areas, work areas, etc.

Condition class—The attributes used to subdivide (called mapping) P2 and P3 sample plots that straddle more than one homogeneous condition. This mapping into homogeneous conditions is done in two phases: (1) the first map delineation identifies if forest or nonforest, and (2) if forest, the plot is mapped according to the following condition classes when present: forest type, stand origin, stand size, owner group, reserve status, and stand density.

D.b.h. (diameter at breast height)—Tree diameter in inches (outside bark) at breast height (4.5 feet aboveground).

D.o.b. (diameter outside bark)—Stem diameter including bark.

Erosion—The wearing away of the land surface by running water, wind, ice, or other geological agents.

Forest industry land—See ownership.

Forest land—Land at least 10 percent stocked by forest trees of any size, or formerly having had such tree cover, and not currently developed for nonforest use. The minimum area considered for classification is 1 acre. Forested strips must be at least 120 feet wide.

Forest management type—A classification of timberland based on forest type and stand origin.

Planted pine—Stands that (1) have been artificially regenerated by planting or direct seeding, (2) are classed as a pine or other softwood forest type, and (3) have at least 10 percent stocking.

Natural pine—Stands that (1) have not been artificially regenerated, (2) are classed as a pine or other softwood forest type, and (3) have at least 10 percent stocking.

Oak-pine—Stands that have at least 10 percent stocking and classed as a forest type of oak-pine.

Upland hardwood—Stands that have at least 10 percent stocking and classed as an oak-hickory or maple-beech-birch forest type.

Lowland hardwood—Stands that have at least 10 percent stocking with a forest type of oak-gum-cypress, elm-ash-cottonwood, palm, or other tropical.

Nonstocked stands—Stands <10 percent stocked with live trees.

Forest-type group (FTG)—A grouping of several detailed forest types. The grouping is based on forest types with similar physiographic and physiognomic characteristics.

Eastern redcedar—Forests in which eastern redcedar constitutes a plurality of the stocking. (Common associates in east Oklahoma, include shortleaf pine, loblolly pine, and oaks.)

Elm-ash-cottonwood—Forests in which elm, ash, or cottonwood, singly or in combination, constitute a plurality of the stocking. (Common associates include willow, sycamore, beech, and maple.)

Loblolly-shortleaf pine—Forests in which loblolly pine, shortleaf pine, or other southern yellow pines, except longleaf or slash pine, singly or in combination, constitute a plurality of the stocking. (Common associates include oak, hickory, and gum.)

Oak-gum-cypress—Bottomland forests in which tupelo, blackgum, sweetgum, oaks, or southern cypress, singly or in combination, constitute a plurality of the stocking, except where pines account for 25 to 50 percent of stocking, in which case the stand would be classified as oak-pine. (Common associates include cottonwood, willow, ash, elm, hackberry, and maple.)

Oak-hickory—Forests in which upland oaks or hickory, singly or in combination, constitute a plurality of the stocking, except where pines account for 25 to 50 percent, in which case the stand would be classified oak-pine. (Common associates include yellow-poplar, elm, maple, and black walnut.)

Oak-pine—Forests in which hardwoods (usually upland oaks) constitute a plurality of the stocking but in which pines account for 25 to 50 percent of the stocking. (Common associates include gum, hickory, and yellow-poplar.)

Growing-stock trees—Living trees of commercial species classified as sawtimber, poletimber, saplings, and seedlings. Trees must contain at least one 12-foot or two 8-foot logs in the saw-log portion, currently or potentially (if too small to qualify), to be classed as growing stock. The log(s) must meet dimension and merchantability standards to qualify. Trees must also have, currently or potentially, one-third of the gross board-foot volume in sound wood.

Growing-stock volume—The cubic-foot volume of sound wood in growing-stock trees at least 5.0 inches d.b.h. from a 1-foot stump to a minimum 4.0-inch top d.o.b. of the central stem.

Hot check—An inspection normally done as part of the training process. The inspector is present on the plot with the trainee and provides immediate feedback regarding data quality. Data errors are corrected. Hot checks can be done on training plots or production plots. See QA/QC.

Hardwoods—Dicotyledonous trees, usually broadleaf and deciduous.

Soft hardwoods—Hardwood species with an average specific gravity of ≤0.50, such as gums, yellow-poplar, cottonwoods, red maple, basswoods, and willows.

Hard hardwoods—Hardwood species with an average specific gravity >0.50 such as oaks, hard maples, hickories, and beech.

Hexagonal grid (Hex)—A hexagonal grid formed from equilateral triangles for the purpose of tessellating the FIA inventory sample. Each hexagon in the base grid has an area of 5,937 acres (2402.6 ha) and contains one (phase 2) inventory plot. The base grid can be subdivided into smaller hexagons to intensify the sample.

Land area—The area of dry land and land temporarily or partly covered by water, such as marshes, swamps, and river floodplains (omitting tidal flats below mean high tide), streams, sloughs, estuaries, and canals <200-feet wide, and lakes, reservoirs, and ponds <4.5 acres in area.

Large-diameter tree—Softwoods ≥9.0 inches d.b.h. and hardwoods ≥11.0 inches d.b.h. These trees were called sawtimber trees in prior surveys. See stand-size class.

Live trees—All living trees ≥5.0 inches in d.b.h. All tree classes, and both commercial and noncommercial species are included. Note: all-live trees include all living trees ≥1.0 inch in d.b.h. Also, see all-live trees, live-tree volume and all-live biomass.

Live-tree volume—Cubic-foot volume of all living trees ≥5.0 inches in d.b.h. All tree classes, and both commercial and noncommercial species are included.

Measurement quality objective (MQO)—An estimate of the precision, bias, and completeness of data necessary to satisfy a prescribed application (e.g., Resource Planning Act). Describes the established tolerance for each data element. MQOs consist of two parts: a statement of the tolerance and a percentage of time when the collected data are required to be within tolerance. Measurement quality objectives can only be assigned where standard methods of sampling or field measurements exist, or where experience has established upper or lower bounds on precision or bias.

Medium-diameter tree—Softwoods 5.0 to 8.9 inches d.b.h. and hardwoods 5.0 to 10.9 inches d.b.h. These trees were called poletimber trees in prior surveys. See stand-size class.

National forest land—See ownership.

Net annual change—Increase or decrease in stand volume of growing stock or live trees ≥5.0 inches d.b.h. Net annual change is equal to net annual growth minus average annual removals.

Net annual growth—Increase in stand volume of growing stock or live trees ≥5.0 inches d.b.h. Net annual growth is equal to gross growth minus mortality.

Noncensus water—A nonforest classification used by FIA to identify water bodies that are 1 to 4.5 acres, or water courses 30 to 200 feet in width, sizes that are below the thresholds used by the U.S. Census.

Noncommercial species—Tree species of typically small size, poor form, or inferior quality that normally do not develop into trees suitable for industrial wood products.

Nonforest land—Land that has never supported forests and land formerly forested where establishment of trees is precluded by development for other uses.

Nonindustrial private forest (NIPF)—See ownership.

Nonstocked stands—Stands <10 percent stocked with live trees.

Other forest land—Forest land other than timberland and productive reserved forest land. It includes available and reserved forest land which is incapable of producing 20 cubic feet per acre per year of industrial wood under natural conditions, because of adverse site conditions such as sterile soils, dry climate, poor drainage, high elevation, steepness, or rockiness. Called woodland or unproductive forest land in previous reports.

Other public land—See ownership.

Ownership—The property owned by one ownership unit, including all parcels of land in the United States.

National forest land—Federal land that has been legally designated as national forests or purchase units, and other land under the administration of the Forest Service, including experimental areas and Bankhead-Jones Title III land.

Forest industry land—Land owned by companies or individuals operating primary wood-using plants.

Nonindustrial private forest land—Privately owned land excluding forest industry land.

Corporate—Owned by corporations, including incorporated farm ownerships.

Individual—All lands owned by individuals, including farm operators.

Other public—An ownership class that includes all public lands except national forests.

Miscellaneous Federal land—Federal land other than national forests.

State, county, and municipal land—Land owned by States, counties, and local public agencies or municipalities or land leased to these governmental units for ≥50 years.

Phase 1 (P1)—Forest Inventory and Analysis activities related to remote sensing, the primary purpose of which is to label plots and obtain stratum weights for population estimates.

Phase 2 (P2)—Forest Inventory and Analysis activities conducted on the network of ground plots. The primary purpose is to obtain field data that enable classification and summarization of area, tree, and other attributes associated with forest land uses.

Phase 3 (P3)—Forest Inventory and Analysis activities conducted on a subset of Phase 2 plots. Additional attributes related to forest health are measured on phase 3 plots (P3 plots were not measured for this cycle).

Plantation or planted stands—Stands that currently show evidence of being planted or artificially seeded. See stand origin.

Plot condition—See condition class.

Poletimber-size trees—Softwoods 5.0 to 8.9 inches d.b.h. and hardwoods 5.0 to 10.9 inches d.b.h. Now called medium-diameter tree.

Productive-reserved forest land—Forest land sufficiently productive to qualify as timberland but withdrawn from timber utilization through statute or administrative regulation.

Quality assurance (QA)—The total integrated program for ensuring that the uncertainties inherent in Forest Inventory and Analysis data are known and do not exceed acceptable magnitudes, within a stated level of confidence. Quality assurance encompasses the plans, specifications, and policies affecting the collection, processing, and reporting of data. It is the system of activities designed to provide program managers and project leaders with independent assurance that total system quality control is being effectively implemented.

Quality control (QC)—The routine application of prescribed field and laboratory procedures (e.g., random check cruising, periodic calibration, instrument maintenance, use of certified standards, etc.) in order to reduce random and systematic errors and ensure that data are generated within known and acceptable performance limits. Quality control also ensures the use of qualified personnel; reliable equipment and supplies; training of personnel; good field and laboratory practices; and strict adherence to standard operating procedures.

Rotten trees—Live trees of commercial species not containing at least one 12-foot saw log, or two noncontiguous saw logs, each ≥8 feet, now or prospectively, primarily because of rot or missing sections, and with less than one-third of the gross board-foot tree volume in sound material.

Rough trees—Live trees of commercial species not containing at least one 12-foot saw log, or two noncontiguous saw logs, each ≥8 feet, now or prospectively, primarily because of roughness, poor form, splits, and cracks, and with less than one-third of the gross board-foot tree volume in sound material; and live trees of noncommercial species.

Sampling error—The standard error of the mean expressed as a percentage. This percentage format allows the application of confidence intervals to the population values (the most common values presented in FIA reports). Most FIA sampling errors are presented at the 0.6827 level but the 0.95 level can easily be obtained by multiplying the sampling error by 1.96, or higher appropriate t-value if n is <120 (Rohlf and Sokal 1969). In this report, all graphs with confidence interval bars are presented at the 0.95 level of confidence; the sampling errors in tables B.3 and B.4 are presented at the 0.6827 confidence level.

Sapling—Live trees 1.0 to 4.9 inches in diameter. Now called small-diameter tree. See stand-size class.

Saw log—A log meeting minimum standards of diameter, length, and defect, including logs at least 8-feet long, sound and straight, with a minimum diameter inside bark for softwoods of 6 inches (8 inches for hardwoods).

Saw-log portion—The part of the bole of sawtimber trees between a 1-foot stump and the saw-log top.

Sawtimber-size trees—Softwoods ≥9.0 inches d.b.h. and hardwoods ≥11.0 inches d.b.h. Now called large-diameter trees.

Sawtimber volume—Growing-stock volume in the saw-log portion of saw-timber-size trees in board feet (International ¼-inch rule). Includes qualifying softwood trees ≥9.0 inches in d.b.h. and qualifying hardwood trees ≥11.0 inches in d.b.h. See volume of sawtimber.

Seedlings—Trees <1.0-inch d.b.h. and >1-foot tall for hardwoods, >6 inches tall for softwoods, and >0.5 inch in diameter at ground level for longleaf pine. Now called small-diameter tree. See stand-size class.

Select red oaks—A group of several red oak species composed of cherrybark, Shumard, and northern red oaks. Other red oak species are included in the "other red oaks" group.

Select white oaks—A group of several white oak species composed of white, swamp chestnut, swamp white, chinkapin, Durand, and bur oaks. Other white oak species are included in the "other white oaks" group.

Site class—A classification of forest land in terms of potential capacity to grow crops of industrial wood based on fully stocked natural stands.

Small-diameter tree—Trees <5.0 inches in d.b.h. These trees were called saplings (trees 1.0 to 4.9 inches in d.b.h.) or seedlings (trees <1.0-inch d.b.h. and >1-foot tall for hardwoods; >6 inches tall for softwoods, and >0.5 inch in d.b.h. at ground level for longleaf pine) in prior surveys. See stand-size class.

Softwoods—Coniferous trees, usually evergreen, having leaves that are needles or scale-like.

Yellow pines—Loblolly, longleaf, slash, pond, shortleaf, pitch, Virginia, sand, spruce, and Table Mountain pines.

Other softwoods—Cypress, eastern redcedar, white-cedar, eastern white pine, eastern hemlock, spruce, and fir.

Stand age—The average age of dominant and codominant trees in the stand.

Stand origin—A classification of forest stands describing their means of origin.

Planted—Planted or artificially seeded.

Natural—No evidence of artificial regeneration.

Stand-size class—A classification of forest land based on the diameter-class distribution of live trees in the stand. See definitions of large tree, medium tree, and small trees.

Large-diameter stands—Stands at least 10 percent stocked with live trees, with one-half or more of total stocking in large and medium trees, and with large-tree stocking at least equal to medium-tree stocking. Called sawtimber in previous reports.

Medium-diameter stands—Stands at least 10 percent stocked with live trees, with one-half or more of total stocking in medium and large trees, and with medium-tree stocking exceeding large-tree stocking. Called poletimber in previous reports.

Small-diameter stands—Stands at least 10 percent stocked with live trees, in which small trees and seedlings account for more than one-half of total stocking. Called sapling-seedling in previous reports.

Nonstocked stands—Stands <10 percent stocked with live trees.

Stocking—The degree of occupancy of land by trees. The stocking value is based on the basal area or the number of trees in a stand as compared to a minimum specified stocking standard. Stocking standard used by FIA; density of trees and basal area per acre required for full stocking:

D.b.h. class	Trees per acre for full stocking	Basal area
inches		square feet per acre
Seedlings	600	—
2	560	—
4	460	—
6	340	67
8	240	84
10	155	85
12	115	90
14	90	96
16	72	101
18	60	106
20	51	111

— = not applicable.

Stocking class—All-live tree stocking classes, including seedlings.

Overstocked—Stands with ≥100 percent stocking.

Fully stocked—Stands with 60 to 99 percent stocking.

Medium stocked—Stands with 35 to 59 percent stocking.

Poorly stocked—Stands with 10 to 34 percent stocking.

Nonstocked—Stands with 0 to 9 percent stocking.

Timberland—Forest land capable of producing 20 cubic feet, or more, of industrial wood per acre per year and not withdrawn from timber utilization. Timberland is synonymous with "commercial forest land" in earlier reports.

Tree—Woody plant having one erect perennial stem or trunk at least 3 inches d.b.h., a more or less definitely formed crown of foliage, and a height of at least 13 feet (at maturity).

Tree class—An assessment of the general quality of a tree. Three classes are recognized: growing stock, rough, and rotten. See definitions for these types of trees.

Tree grade—A classification of the saw-log portion of sawtimber trees based on: (1) the grade of the butt log, or (2) the ability to produce at least one 12-foot or two 8-foot logs in the upper section of the saw-log portion. Tree grade is an indicator of quality; grade 1 is the best quality.

Unproductive forest land—See other forest land.

Volume of live trees—The cubic-foot volume of sound wood in live trees ≥5.0 inches d.b.h. from a 1-foot stump to a minimum 4.0-inch bole top d.o.b. of the central stem.

Volume of sawtimber trees (in saw-log portion)—The cubic-foot volume (International ¼-inch rule) of sound wood in the saw-log portion of sawtimber trees (from a 1-foot stump to a log top minimum of 7.0 inches d.o.b. for softwoods; from a 1-foot stump to a log top minimum of 9.0 inches d.o.b. for hardwoods). Volume is the net result after deductions for rot, sweep, and other defects that affect use for lumber. Sawtimber trees are growing-stock trees that meet the minimum size requirements. See definition for growing-stock trees.

Woodland—See other forest land.

Table A.1—Percentage of area by land status, east Oklahoma, 2008

Land status	Area
	percent
Accessible forest land	
Unreserved forest land	
Timberland	48.3
Unproductive	5.6
Total	53.9
Reserved forest land	
Productive	0.5
Unproductive	0.0
Total	0.5
Total forest land	54.4
Nonforest and other area	
Nonforest land	41.1
Water	
Noncensus water	0.5
Census water	4.0
Total	45.6
Nonsampled area	
Access denied	1.0
Hazardous conditions	0.0
All area	100.0
Total area *(thousand acres)*	10,450.7

Numbers in rows and columns may not sum to totals due to rounding.
0.0 = no sample for the cell or a value of > 0.0 but < 0.05.

Table A.1.1—Area by survey unit and land status, east Oklahoma, 2008

Survey unit	Total area	All forest	Unreserved			Reserved			Nonforest land	Census water
			Total	Timber-land	Unpro-ductive	Total	Productive	Unpro-ductive		
					thousand acres					
Southeast	6,988.6	4,207.0	4,160.5	3,725.1	435.5	46.5	46.5	0.0	2,560.8	220.8
Northeast	3,571.4	1,538.0	1,533.7	1,378.0	155.7	4.3	4.3	0.0	1,830.6	202.9
All units	10,560.0	5,745.0	5,694.2	5,103.1	591.1	50.8	50.8	0.0	4,391.4	423.7

Numbers in rows and columns may not sum to totals due to rounding.
0.0 = no sample for the cell or a value of > 0.0 but < 0.05.

Table A.2—Area of forest land by ownership class and land status, east Oklahoma, 2008

Ownership class	All forest land	Unreserved			Reserved		
		Total	Timber-land	Unpro-ductive	Total	Productive	Unpro-ductive
				thousand acres			
U.S. Forest Service							
National forest	286.4	263.3	257.5	5.8	23.1	23.1	0.0
Total	286.4	263.3	257.5	5.8	23.1	23.1	0.0
Other Federal							
U.S. Fish and Wildlife Service	9.3	9.3	9.3	0.0	0.0	0.0	0.0
Dept. of Defense/Dept. of Energy	246.6	246.6	225.1	21.5	0.0	0.0	0.0
Other Federal	62.2	62.2	62.2	0.0	0.0	0.0	0.0
Total	318.1	318.1	296.6	21.5	0.0	0.0	0.0
State and local government							
State	176.6	149.0	136.5	12.5	27.7	27.7	0.0
Local	34.2	34.2	27.6	6.6	0.0	0.0	0.0
Total	210.9	183.2	164.1	19.1	27.7	27.7	0.0
Forest industry							
Corporate	568.3	568.3	568.3	0.0	0.0	0.0	0.0
Total	568.3	568.3	568.3	0.0	0.0	0.0	0.0
Nonindustrial private							
Corporate	828.4	828.4	765.7	62.8	0.0	0.0	0.0
Conservation/natural resources organization	11.8	11.8	11.8	0.0	0.0	0.0	0.0
Unincorporated partnership/ association/club	136.7	136.7	113.8	22.9	0.0	0.0	0.0
Native American	49.9	49.9	49.9	0.0	0.0	0.0	0.0
Individual	3,334.4	3,334.4	2,875.3	459.1	0.0	0.0	0.0
Total	4,361.3	4,361.3	3,816.5	544.8	0.0	0.0	0.0
All classes	5,745.0	5,694.2	5,103.1	591.1	50.8	50.8	0.0

Numbers in rows and columns may not sum to totals due to rounding.
0.0 = no sample for the cell or a value of > 0.0 but < 0.05.

Table A.3—Area of forest land by forest-type group and site productivity class, east Oklahoma, 2008

Forest-type group	All classes	Site productivity class *(cubic feet/acre/year)*						
		0–19	20–49	50–84	85–119	120–164	165–224	225+
		thousand acres						
Softwood								
Loblolly-shortleaf pine	1,080.1	0.0	191.5	588.5	216.8	83.3	0.0	0.0
Other eastern softwoods	44.4	4.3	27.7	12.4	0.0	0.0	0.0	0.0
Pinyon-juniper	1.2	1.2	0.0	0.0	0.0	0.0	0.0	0.0
Total softwoods	1,125.7	5.6	219.2	600.9	216.8	83.3	0.0	0.0
Hardwood								
Oak-pine	601.3	59.7	145.0	321.5	47.1	22.2	5.8	0.0
Oak-hickory	3,462.6	525.7	1,778.8	961.2	128.7	41.8	26.4	0.0
Oak-gum-cypress	141.5	0.0	27.3	55.6	35.8	16.7	6.0	0.0
Elm-ash-cottonwood	369.8	0.2	96.6	200.6	56.7	5.8	3.5	6.4
Other hardwoods	8.8	0.0	0.0	8.8	0.0	0.0	0.0	0.0
Total hardwoods	4,584.0	585.5	2,047.7	1,547.8	268.3	86.5	41.7	6.4
Nonstocked	35.3	0.0	20.1	12.2	0.0	1.4	1.5	0.0
All groups	5,745.0	591.1	2,287.1	2,160.9	485.1	171.2	43.2	6.4

Numbers in rows and columns may not sum to totals due to rounding.
0.0 = no sample for the cell or a value of > 0.0 but < 0.05.

Table A.3.1—Area of timberland by forest-type group and site productivity class, east Oklahoma, 2008

Forest-type group	All classes	Site productivity class *(cubic feet/acre/year)*						
		0–19	20–49	50–84	85–119	120–164	165–224	225+
		thousand acres						
Softwood								
Loblolly-shortleaf pine	1,056.7	0.0	191.5	576.9	205.0	83.3	0.0	0.0
Other eastern softwoods	40.1	0.0	27.7	12.4	0.0	0.0	0.0	0.0
Total softwoods	1,096.8	0.0	219.2	589.3	205.0	83.3	0.0	0.0
Hardwood								
Oak-pine	530.1	0.0	139.3	315.7	47.1	22.2	5.8	0.0
Oak-hickory	2,921.0	0.0	1,773.0	951.1	128.7	41.8	26.4	0.0
Oak-gum-cypress	141.5	0.0	27.3	55.6	35.8	16.7	6.0	0.0
Elm-ash-cottonwood	369.6	0.0	96.6	200.6	56.7	5.8	3.5	6.4
Other hardwoods	8.8	0.0	0.0	8.8	0.0	0.0	0.0	0.0
Total hardwoods	3,971.0	0.0	2,036.2	1,532.0	268.3	86.5	41.7	6.4
Nonstocked	35.3	0.0	20.1	12.2	0.0	1.4	1.5	0.0
All groups	5,103.1	0.0	2,275.5	2,133.5	473.3	171.2	43.2	6.4

Numbers in rows and columns may not sum to totals due to rounding.
0.0 = no sample for the cell or a value of > 0.0 but < 0.05.

Table A.4—Area of forest land by forest-type group and ownership group, east Oklahoma, 2008

Forest-type group	All ownerships	U.S. Forest Service	Other federal	State and local government	Forest industry	Nonindustrial private
				thousand acres		
Softwood						
Loblolly-shortleaf pine	1,080.1	169.3	45.4	34.9	350.6	479.9
Other eastern softwoods	44.4	1.4	5.8	5.8	0.0	31.4
Pinyon-juniper	1.2	0.0	0.0	0.0	0.0	1.2
Total softwoods	1,125.7	170.8	51.1	40.7	350.6	512.5
Hardwood						
Oak-pine	601.3	31.7	5.5	24.6	81.2	458.3
Oak-hickory	3,462.6	83.9	164.7	124.0	123.9	2,966.1
Oak-gum-cypress	141.5	0.0	40.5	6.2	1.4	93.3
Elm-ash-cottonwood	369.8	0.0	54.8	15.4	8.4	291.3
Other hardwoods	8.8	0.0	0.0	0.0	0.0	8.8
Total hardwoods	4,584.0	115.6	265.5	170.2	214.8	3,817.8
Nonstocked	35.3	0.0	1.4	0.0	2.9	31.0
All groups	5,745.0	286.4	318.1	210.9	568.3	4,361.3

Numbers in rows and columns may not sum to totals due to rounding.
0.0 = no sample for the cell or a value of > 0.0 but < 0.05.

Table A.4.1—Area of timberland by forest-type group and ownership group, east Oklahoma, 2008

Forest-type group	All ownerships	U.S. Forest Service	Other Federal	State and local government	Forest industry	Nonindustrial private
				thousand acres		
Softwood						
Loblolly-shortleaf pine	1,056.7	157.7	45.4	23.1	350.6	479.9
Other eastern softwoods	40.1	1.4	5.8	5.8	0.0	27.1
Total softwoods	1,096.8	159.2	51.1	28.9	350.6	507.0
Hardwood						
Oak-pine	530.1	20.2	5.5	18.8	81.2	404.4
Oak-hickory	2,921.0	78.1	143.2	95.0	123.9	2,480.8
Oak-gum-cypress	141.5	0.0	40.5	6.2	1.4	93.3
Elm-ash-cottonwood	369.6	0.0	54.8	15.2	8.4	291.3
Other hardwoods	8.8	0.0	0.0	0.0	0.0	8.8
Total hardwoods	3,971.0	98.3	244.0	135.2	214.8	3,278.6
Nonstocked	35.3	0.0	1.4	0.0	2.9	31.0
All groups	5,103.1	257.5	296.6	164.1	568.3	3,816.5

Numbers in rows and columns may not sum to totals due to rounding.
0.0 = no sample for the cell or a value of > 0.0 but < 0.05.

Table A.5—Area of forest land by forest-type group and stand-size class, east Oklahoma, 2008

Forest-type group	All size classes	Stand-size class			
		Large diameter	Medium diameter	Small diameter	Non-stocked
		thousand acres			
Softwood					
Loblolly-shortleaf pine	1,080.1	630.9	252.7	196.5	0.0
Other eastern softwoods	44.4	8.5	22.2	13.7	0.0
Pinyon-juniper	1.2	0.0	1.2	0.0	0.0
Total softwoods	1,125.7	639.4	276.1	210.3	0.0
Hardwood					
Oak-pine	601.3	194.8	247.8	158.7	0.0
Oak-hickory	3,462.6	1,157.9	1,456.3	848.3	0.0
Oak-gum-cypress	141.5	80.0	33.4	28.0	0.0
Elm-ash-cottonwood	369.8	207.5	91.8	70.5	0.0
Other hardwoods	8.8	0.0	4.3	4.5	0.0
Total hardwoods	4,584.0	1,640.2	1,833.7	1,110.0	0.0
Nonstocked	35.3	0.0	0.0	0.0	35.3
All groups	5,745.0	2,279.6	2,109.8	1,320.3	35.3

Numbers in rows and columns may not sum to totals due to rounding.
0.0 = no sample for the cell or a value of > 0.0 but < 0.05.

Table A.6—Area of forest land by forest-type group and stand age class, east Oklahoma, 2008

Forest-type group	All classes	1–20	21–40	41–60	61–80	81–100	101–120	121–140	141–160	161–180	181–200	201+	Non-stocked
							thousand acres						
Softwood													
Loblolly-shortleaf pine	1,080.1	341.6	373.0	245.6	98.0	15.9	6.0	0.0	0.0	0.0	0.0	0.0	0.0
Other eastern softwoods	44.4	8.3	17.9	13.9	4.3	0.0	0.0	0.0	0.0	0.0	0.0	0.0	0.0
Pinyon-juniper	1.2	0.0	0.0	1.2	0.0	0.0	0.0	0.0	0.0	0.0	0.0	0.0	0.0
Total softwoods	1,125.7	349.9	390.9	260.7	102.3	15.9	6.0	0.0	0.0	0.0	0.0	0.0	0.0
Hardwood													
Oak-pine	601.3	123.6	118.8	198.1	126.8	28.2	0.0	5.8	0.0	0.0	0.0	0.0	0.0
Oak-hickory	3,462.6	665.6	564.9	1,085.2	920.7	196.4	24.0	0.0	0.0	0.0	0.0	0.0	5.8
Oak-gum-cypress	141.5	22.2	47.5	40.7	20.8	10.2	0.0	0.0	0.0	0.0	0.0	0.0	0.0
Elm-ash-cottonwood	369.8	98.0	80.3	108.5	70.9	8.0	4.1	0.0	0.0	0.0	0.0	0.0	0.0
Other hardwoods	8.8	4.5	4.3	0.0	0.0	0.0	0.0	0.0	0.0	0.0	0.0	0.0	0.0
Total hardwoods	4,584.0	914.0	815.8	1,432.5	1,139.3	242.8	28.1	5.8	0.0	0.0	0.0	0.0	5.8
Nonstocked	35.3	0.0	0.0	0.0	0.0	0.0	0.0	0.0	0.0	0.0	0.0	0.0	35.3
All groups	5,745.0	1,263.9	1,206.6	1,693.2	1,241.6	258.7	34.2	5.8	0.0	0.0	0.0	0.0	41.1

Numbers in rows and columns may not sum to totals due to rounding.
0.0 = no sample for the cell or a value of > 0.0 but < 0.05.

Table A.6.1—Area of timberland by forest-type group and stand age class, east Oklahoma, 2008

Forest-type group	All classes	Stand age (years)											Non-stocked
		1–10	11–20	21–30	31–40	41–50	51–60	61–70	71–80	81–90	91–100	101+	
		thousand acres											
Softwood													
Loblolly-shortleaf pine	1,056.7	198.8	142.8	277.6	95.4	113.9	131.6	74.6	11.8	4.3	5.8	0.0	0.0
Other eastern softwoods	40.1	0.0	8.3	16.4	1.6	1.4	12.5	0.0	0.0	0.0	0.0	0.0	0.0
Total softwoods	1,096.8	198.8	151.1	294.0	96.9	115.4	144.1	74.6	11.8	4.3	5.8	0.0	0.0
Hardwood													
Oak-pine	530.1	83.9	33.5	40.6	65.8	92.5	92.1	75.9	28.4	11.6	0.0	5.8	0.0
Oak-hickory	2,921.0	334.7	271.1	242.1	274.4	407.2	499.2	542.5	206.2	108.1	24.1	5.8	5.8
Oak-gum-cypress	141.5	11.9	10.4	14.6	32.8	24.7	16.1	11.6	9.3	10.2	0.0	0.0	0.0
Elm-ash-cottonwood	369.6	40.0	57.8	35.2	45.0	42.0	66.5	63.4	7.4	6.4	1.6	4.1	0.0
Other hardwoods	8.8	0.0	4.5	4.3	0.0	0.0	0.0	0.0	0.0	0.0	0.0	0.0	0.0
Total hardwoods	3,971.0	470.4	377.3	336.9	418.0	566.4	673.9	693.4	251.3	136.3	25.7	15.7	5.8
Nonstocked	35.3	0.0	0.0	0.0	0.0	0.0	0.0	0.0	0.0	0.0	0.0	0.0	35.3
All groups	5,103.1	669.2	528.4	630.8	514.9	681.8	818.0	768.0	263.1	140.6	31.5	15.7	41.1

Numbers in rows and columns may not sum to totals due to rounding.

0.0 = no sample for the cell or a value of > 0.0 but < 0.05.

Table A.7—Area of forest land by forest-type group and stand origin, east Oklahoma, 2008

Forest-type group	Total	Stand origin Natural stands	Stand origin Artificial regeneration
		thousand acres	
Softwood			
Loblolly-shortleaf pine	1,080.1	495.0	585.1
Other eastern softwoods	44.4	44.4	0.0
Pinyon-juniper	1.2	1.2	0.0
Total softwoods	1,125.7	540.7	585.1
Hardwood			
Oak-pine	601.3	536.8	64.5
Oak-hickory	3,462.6	3,431.2	31.3
Oak-gum-cypress	141.5	141.5	0.0
Elm-ash-cottonwood	369.8	368.3	1.5
Other hardwoods	8.8	8.8	0.0
Total hardwoods	4,584.0	4,486.6	97.4
Nonstocked	35.3	33.8	1.4
All groups	5,745.0	5,061.1	683.9

Numbers in rows and columns may not sum to totals due to rounding.
0.0 = no sample for the cell or a value of > 0.0 but < 0.05.

Table A.7.1—Area of timberland by forest-type group and stand origin, east Oklahoma, 2008

Forest-type group	Total	Stand origin Natural stands	Stand origin Artificial regeneration
		thousand acres	
Softwood			
Loblolly-shortleaf pine	1,056.7	471.6	585.1
Other eastern softwoods	40.1	40.1	0.0
Total softwoods	1,096.8	511.7	585.1
Hardwood			
Oak-pine	530.1	471.8	58.3
Oak-hickory	2,921.0	2,889.6	31.3
Oak-gum-cypress	141.5	141.5	0.0
Elm-ash-cottonwood	369.6	368.1	1.5
Other hardwoods	8.8	8.8	0.0
Total hardwoods	3,971.0	3,879.8	91.2
Nonstocked	35.3	33.8	1.4
All groups	5,103.1	4,425.4	677.7

Numbers in rows and columns may not sum to totals due to rounding.
0.0 = no sample for the cell or a value of > 0.0 but < 0.05.

Table A.8—Area of forest land disturbed annually[a] by forest-type group and disturbance class, east Oklahoma, 2008

Forest-type group	Disturbance class							
	Insects	Disease	Weather	Fire	Domestic animals	Wild animals	Human	Other natural
	thousand acres							
Softwood								
Loblolly-shortleaf pine	2.1	0.0	5.5	9.4	0.0	0.0	0.9	0.0
Other eastern softwoods	0.0	0.0	0.0	0.0	0.0	0.0	0.0	0.0
Total softwoods	2.1	0.0	5.5	9.4	0.0	0.0	0.9	0.0
Hardwood								
Oak-pine	0.4	0.8	5.6	4.7	0.0	0.4	0.0	0.0
Oak-hickory	0.0	3.3	43.8	33.1	3.5	0.4	4.7	0.0
Oak-gum-cypress	0.0	0.0	4.4	0.9	0.0	0.0	0.9	0.0
Elm-ash-cottonwood	0.0	0.0	6.1	1.4	0.0	2.2	0.8	0.0
Other hardwoods	0.0	0.0	0.0	0.0	0.0	0.0	0.0	0.0
Total hardwoods	0.4	4.2	59.9	40.0	3.5	3.0	6.4	0.0
Nonstocked	0.0	0.0	0.0	0.0	0.0	0.0	0.0	0.0
All groups	2.5	4.2	65.4	49.4	3.5	3.0	7.3	0.0

Numbers in rows and columns may not sum to totals due to rounding.

0.0 = no sample for the cell or a value of > 0.0 but < 0.05.

[a] The area disturbed annually is based on the forest-type group that was present at the end of the previous survey (the forest-type group present before the disturbance occurred).

Table A.8.1—Area of timberland disturbed annually[a] by forest-type group and disturbance class, east Oklahoma, 2008

Forest-type group	Disturbance class							
	Insects	Disease	Weather	Fire	Domestic animals	Wild animals	Human	Other natural
	thousand acres							
Softwood								
Loblolly-shortleaf pine	2.1	0.0	5.5	8.5	0.0	0.0	0.9	0.0
Other eastern softwoods	0.0	0.0	0.0	0.0	0.0	0.0	0.0	0.0
Total softwoods	2.1	0.0	5.5	8.5	0.0	0.0	0.9	0.0
Hardwood								
Oak-pine	0.4	0.8	5.6	4.3	0.0	0.4	0.0	0.0
Oak-hickory	0.0	2.1	35.7	26.3	3.1	0.4	3.9	0.0
Oak-gum-cypress	0.0	0.0	4.4	0.9	0.0	0.0	0.9	0.0
Elm-ash-cottonwood	0.0	0.0	6.1	1.4	0.0	2.2	0.8	0.0
Other hardwoods	0.0	0.0	0.0	0.0	0.0	0.0	0.0	0.0
Total hardwoods	0.4	2.9	51.8	32.8	3.1	3.0	5.6	0.0
Nonstocked	0.0	0.0	0.0	0.0	0.0	0.0	0.0	0.0
All groups	2.5	2.9	57.3	41.3	3.1	3.0	6.4	0.0

Numbers in rows and columns may not sum to totals due to rounding.

0.0 = no sample for the cell or a value of > 0.0 but < 0.05.

[a] The area disturbed annually is based on the forest-type group that was present at the end of the previous survey (the forest-type group present before the disturbance occurred).

Table A.8.2—Area of forest land treated annually[a] by forest-type group and treatment class, east Oklahoma, 2008

Forest-type group				Treatment class						
			Cutting							
	Total treated	Final harvest	Partial harvest	Seed-tree/ shelter-wood harvest	Com-mercial thinning	Timber stand improve-ment	Site prepa-ration	Artificial regen-eration	Natural regen-eration	Other silvi-cultural
					thousand acres					
Softwood										
Loblolly-shortleaf pine	46.0	19.2	11.1	0.9	14.5	0.4	14.0	14.0	5.6	0.4
Oher eastern softwoods	0.0	0.0	0.0	0.0	0.0	0.0	0.0	0.0	0.0	0.0
Total softwoods	46.0	19.2	11.1	0.9	14.5	0.4	14.0	14.0	5.6	0.4
Hardwood										
Oak-pine	20.9	5.6	11.5	0.0	3.4	0.4	2.6	3.9	1.8	1.3
Oak-hickory	35.1	9.8	21.7	0.0	3.6	0.0	3.4	5.1	6.1	2.2
Oak-gum-cypress	2.9	0.9	2.1	0.0	0.0	0.0	0.0	0.0	0.0	0.0
Elm-ash-cottonwood	0.8	0.4	0.4	0.0	0.0	0.0	0.0	0.0	0.0	0.0
Other hardwoods	0.0	0.0	0.0	0.0	0.0	0.0	0.0	0.0	0.0	0.0
Total hardwoods	59.8	16.7	35.7	0.0	7.0	0.4	6.0	9.0	7.8	3.5
Nonstocked	0.0	0.0	0.0	0.0	0.0	0.0	0.0	0.0	0.0	0.0
All groups	105.8	35.8	46.8	0.9	21.4	0.9	20.0	23.0	13.5	3.9

Numbers in rows and columns may not sum to totals due to rounding.

0.0 = no sample for the cell or a value of > 0.0 but < 0.05.

[a] The area treated annually is based on the forest-type group that was present at the end of the previous survey (the forest-type group present before the treatment occurred).

Table A.8.3—Area of timberland treated annually[a] by forest-type group and treatment class, east Oklahoma, 2008

				Treatment class						
			Cutting							
Forest-type group	Total treated	Final harvest	Partial harvest	Seed-tree/ shelter-wood harvest	Com-mercial thinning	Timber stand improve-ment	Site prepa-ration	Artificial regen-eration	Natural regen-eration	Other silvi-cultural
					thousand acres					
Softwood										
Loblolly-shortleaf pine	45.1	18.7	11.1	0.9	14.5	0.0	14.0	13.5	5.6	0.4
Oher eastern softwoods	0.0	0.0	0.0	0.0	0.0	0.0	0.0	0.0	0.0	0.0
Total softwoods	45.1	18.7	11.1	0.9	14.5	0.0	14.0	13.5	5.6	0.4
Hardwood										
Oak-pine	20.5	5.6	11.1	0.0	3.4	0.4	2.6	3.9	1.8	1.3
Oak-hickory	32.4	8.9	20.4	0.0	3.1	0.0	3.0	5.1	4.8	1.7
Oak-gum-cypress	2.9	0.9	2.1	0.0	0.0	0.0	0.0	0.0	0.0	0.0
Elm-ash-cottonwood	0.8	0.4	0.4	0.0	0.0	0.0	0.0	0.0	0.0	0.0
Other hardwoods	0.0	0.0	0.0	0.0	0.0	0.0	0.0	0.0	0.0	0.0
Total hardwoods	56.7	15.8	33.9	0.0	6.5	0.4	5.6	9.0	6.5	3.0
Nonstocked	0.0	0.0	0.0	0.0	0.0	0.0	0.0	0.0	0.0	0.0
All groups	101.9	34.5	45.1	0.9	21.0	0.4	19.6	22.5	12.2	3.5

Numbers in rows and columns may not sum to totals due to rounding.

0.0 = no sample for the cell or a value of > 0.0 but < 0.05.

[a] The area treated annually is based on the forest-type group that was present at the end of the previous survey (the forest-type group present before the treatment occurred).

Table A.9—Area of timberland by forest-type group and stand-size class, east Oklahoma, 2008

		Stand-size class			
Forest-type group	All size classes	Large diameter	Medium diameter	Small diameter	Non-stocked
			thousand acres		
Softwood					
Loblolly-shortleaf pine	1,056.7	607.4	252.7	196.5	0.0
Other eastern softwoods	40.1	8.5	17.8	13.7	0.0
Total softwoods	1,096.8	616.0	270.5	210.3	0.0
Hardwood					
Oak-pine	530.1	194.8	196.4	138.9	0.0
Oak-hickory	2,921.0	1,064.8	1,092.4	763.7	0.0
Oak-gum-cypress	141.5	80.0	33.4	28.0	0.0
Elm-ash-cottonwood	369.6	207.5	91.8	70.3	0.0
Other hardwoods	8.8	0.0	4.3	4.5	0.0
Total hardwoods	3,971.0	1,547.1	1,418.4	1,005.5	0.0
Nonstocked	35.3	0.0	0.0	0.0	35.3
All groups	5,103.1	2,163.1	1,688.9	1,215.8	35.3

Numbers in rows and columns may not sum to totals due to rounding.

0.0 = no sample for the cell or a value of > 0.0 but < 0.05.

Table A.10—Number of live trees on forest land by species group and diameter class, east Oklahoma, 2008

Species group[a]	All classes	1.0–2.9	3.0–4.9	5.0–6.9	7.0–8.9	9.0–10.9	11.0–12.9	13.0–14.9	15.0–16.9	17.0–18.9	19.0–20.9	21.0–24.9	25.0–28.9	29.0–32.9	33.0–36.9	37.0+
							million trees									
Softwood																
Loblolly and shortleaf pines	446.6	176.5	101.2	56.1	41.6	27.0	21.8	13.4	5.6	2.3	0.7	0.3	0.0	0.0	0.0	0.0
Cypress	0.0	0.0	0.0	0.0	0.0	0.0	0.0	0.0	0.0	0.0	0.0	0.0	0.0	0.0	0.0	0.0
Other eastern softwoods	155.5	102.0	30.3	13.1	5.9	2.7	0.8	0.5	0.1	0.1	0.0	0.0	0.0	0.0	0.0	0.0
Total softwoods	602.0	278.5	131.5	69.2	47.5	29.7	22.6	13.8	5.8	2.4	0.7	0.3	0.0	0.0	0.0	0.0
Hardwood																
Select white oaks	85.9	36.2	17.9	10.9	7.3	5.7	3.1	2.1	1.2	0.7	0.2	0.4	0.0	0.0	0.0	0.0
Select red oaks	40.8	17.5	9.7	4.0	3.4	2.4	1.3	1.1	0.7	0.4	0.1	0.2	0.0	0.0	0.0	0.0
Other white oaks	450.2	191.4	90.7	69.2	44.1	23.0	13.5	8.6	5.5	2.5	0.8	0.8	0.2	0.0	0.1	0.0
Other red oaks	336.7	190.0	64.9	28.6	18.2	12.4	8.3	5.5	3.0	2.2	1.5	1.3	0.4	0.2	0.1	0.0
Hickory	333.3	205.3	63.2	30.6	15.6	8.1	4.7	2.9	1.4	0.8	0.2	0.4	0.1	0.0	0.0	0.0
Hard maple	8.8	6.1	1.3	0.7	0.2	0.2	0.2	0.0	0.0	0.0	0.0	0.0	0.0	0.0	0.0	0.0
Soft maple	69.4	52.2	11.1	3.1	1.3	0.6	0.1	0.2	0.1	0.3	0.0	0.2	0.0	0.1	0.0	0.0
Beech	2.4	1.9	0.5	0.0	0.0	0.0	0.0	0.0	0.0	0.0	0.0	0.0	0.0	0.0	0.0	0.0
Sweetgum	59.9	36.3	11.9	6.1	2.3	1.5	0.8	0.5	0.2	0.2	0.1	0.0	0.0	0.0	0.0	0.0
Tupelo and blackgum	43.4	30.8	7.6	1.9	1.5	0.6	0.5	0.3	0.1	0.1	0.1	0.0	0.0	0.0	0.0	0.0
Ash	83.6	49.3	15.3	7.1	4.8	3.0	1.9	1.1	0.5	0.2	0.3	0.2	0.0	0.0	0.0	0.0
Cottonwood and aspen	1.2	0.0	0.0	0.2	0.2	0.2	0.2	0.1	0.1	0.2	0.0	0.0	0.0	0.0	0.0	0.0
Basswood	2.4	1.8	0.4	0.1	0.0	0.0	0.0	0.0	0.0	0.0	0.0	0.0	0.0	0.0	0.0	0.0
Black walnut	5.7	1.9	1.4	0.7	0.7	0.3	0.3	0.2	0.1	0.0	0.0	0.0	0.0	0.0	0.0	0.0
Other eastern soft hardwoods	527.4	361.3	100.4	34.0	15.7	7.3	4.2	1.6	1.3	0.5	0.5	0.3	0.1	0.1	0.0	0.0
Other eastern hard hardwoods	141.0	109.8	21.3	5.6	2.5	1.0	0.4	0.3	0.0	0.0	0.0	0.0	0.0	0.0	0.0	0.0
Eastern noncommercial hardwoods	186.2	147.5	26.6	6.8	2.7	1.2	0.7	0.3	0.1	0.1	0.0	0.1	0.1	0.0	0.0	0.0
Western woodland hardwoods	0.2	0.0	0.0	0.0	0.0	0.1	0.1	0.0	0.0	0.0	0.0	0.0	0.0	0.0	0.0	0.0
Total hardwoods	2,378.4	1,439.2	444.2	209.8	120.4	67.5	40.3	24.7	14.1	8.2	3.9	4.0	1.1	0.6	0.3	0.0
All species	2,980.4	1,717.7	575.8	279.0	167.9	97.2	63.0	38.6	19.9	10.6	4.6	4.3	1.1	0.7	0.3	0.0

Numbers in rows and columns may not sum to totals due to rounding.

0.0 = no sample for the cell or a value of > 0.0 but < 0.05.

[a] Palm species have been included (species codes 906 to 915).

Table A.10.1—Number of live trees on timberland by species group and diameter class, east Oklahoma, 2008

Species group[a]	All classes	1.0–2.9	3.0–4.9	5.0–6.9	7.0–8.9	9.0–10.9	11.0–12.9	13.0–14.9	15.0–16.9	17.0–18.9	19.0–20.9	21.0–24.9	25.0–28.9	29.0–32.9	33.0–36.9	37.0+
							Diameter class (inches at breast height)									
							million trees									
Softwood																
Loblolly and shortleaf pines	433.2	172.4	96.2	55.1	40.8	26.1	21.5	12.8	5.3	2.2	0.6	0.2	0.0	0.0	0.0	0.0
Cypress	0.0	0.0	0.0	0.0	0.0	0.0	0.0	0.0	0.0	0.0	0.0	0.0	0.0	0.0	0.0	0.0
Other eastern softwoods	121.7	80.3	22.6	10.5	4.9	2.1	0.6	0.3	0.1	0.1	0.0	0.0	0.0	0.0	0.0	0.0
Total softwoods	554.9	252.8	118.8	65.6	45.7	28.2	22.1	13.1	5.4	2.2	0.6	0.2	0.0	0.0	0.0	0.0
Hardwood																
Select white oaks	81.9	35.7	16.6	10.2	6.9	5.2	2.8	1.9	1.1	0.7	0.2	0.4	0.0	0.0	0.0	0.0
Select red oaks	38.9	17.1	9.2	3.8	3.2	2.0	1.2	0.9	0.6	0.3	0.1	0.2	0.0	0.0	0.0	0.0
Other white oaks	339.7	153.5	61.4	48.4	32.4	18.0	11.0	6.8	4.4	2.0	0.7	0.8	0.2	0.0	0.1	0.0
Other red oaks	297.5	167.6	57.6	24.0	16.1	10.9	7.5	5.1	2.9	2.2	1.5	1.2	0.4	0.2	0.1	0.0
Hickory	290.4	180.7	54.9	25.2	13.2	6.9	4.2	2.6	1.3	0.8	0.2	0.4	0.1	0.0	0.0	0.0
Hard maple	8.7	6.1	1.3	0.7	0.1	0.2	0.1	0.0	0.0	0.0	0.0	0.0	0.0	0.0	0.0	0.0
Soft maple	66.9	51.7	9.3	3.0	1.2	0.6	0.1	0.2	0.1	0.3	0.0	0.2	0.0	0.1	0.0	0.0
Beech	2.4	1.9	0.5	0.0	0.0	0.0	0.0	0.0	0.0	0.0	0.0	0.0	0.0	0.0	0.0	0.0
Sweetgum	59.9	36.3	11.9	6.1	2.3	1.5	0.8	0.5	0.2	0.2	0.1	0.0	0.0	0.0	0.0	0.0
Tupelo and blackgum	42.1	30.3	7.2	1.7	1.3	0.5	0.5	0.3	0.1	0.1	0.1	0.0	0.0	0.0	0.0	0.0
Ash	81.7	48.3	15.3	6.8	4.5	2.9	1.7	1.0	0.5	0.2	0.2	0.2	0.0	0.0	0.0	0.0
Cottonwood and aspen	1.2	0.0	0.0	0.2	0.2	0.2	0.2	0.1	0.1	0.2	0.0	0.0	0.0	0.0	0.0	0.0
Basswood	2.4	1.8	0.4	0.1	0.0	0.0	0.0	0.0	0.0	0.0	0.0	0.0	0.0	0.0	0.0	0.0
Black walnut	5.7	1.9	1.4	0.7	0.7	0.3	0.3	0.2	0.1	0.0	0.0	0.0	0.0	0.0	0.0	0.0
Other eastern soft hardwoods	475.4	325.5	88.7	31.0	14.6	7.0	4.1	1.6	1.3	0.5	0.5	0.3	0.1	0.1	0.0	0.0
Other eastern hard hardwoods	138.8	108.0	21.3	5.4	2.3	1.0	0.4	0.3	0.0	0.0	0.0	0.0	0.0	0.0	0.0	0.0
Eastern noncommercial hardwoods	177.6	140.2	25.6	6.6	2.7	1.2	0.7	0.2	0.1	0.1	0.0	0.1	0.1	0.0	0.0	0.0
Total hardwoods	2,111.1	1,306.7	382.8	173.9	101.8	58.4	35.8	21.9	12.7	7.6	3.7	3.8	1.0	0.6	0.3	0.0
All species	2,666.0	1,559.4	501.6	239.6	147.5	86.6	57.9	35.0	18.1	9.8	4.4	4.1	1.0	0.7	0.3	0.0

Numbers in rows and columns may not sum to totals due to rounding.

0.0 = no sample for the cell or a value of > 0.0 but < 0.05.

[a] Palm species have been included (species codes 906 to 915).

Table A.11—Number of growing-stock trees on timberland by species group and diameter class, east Oklahoma, 2008

Species group[a]	All classes	Diameter class (inches at breast height)												
		5.0–6.9	7.0–8.9	9.0–10.9	11.0–12.9	13.0–14.9	15.0–16.9	17.0–18.9	19.0–20.9	21.0–24.9	25.0–28.9	29.0–32.9	33.0–36.9	37.0+
		million trees												
Softwood														
Loblolly and shortleaf pines	149.8	47.8	37.2	24.7	20.5	11.9	4.8	2.0	0.6	0.2	0.0	0.0	0.0	0.0
Cypress	0.0	0.0	0.0	0.0	0.0	0.0	0.0	0.0	0.0	0.0	0.0	0.0	0.0	0.0
Other eastern softwoods	8.6	4.8	2.4	1.0	0.2	0.1	0.0	0.0	0.0	0.0	0.0	0.0	0.0	0.0
Total softwoods	158.5	52.7	39.6	25.7	20.8	12.1	4.8	2.0	0.6	0.2	0.0	0.0	0.0	0.0
Hardwood														
Select white oaks	21.1	7.3	5.1	4.0	2.0	1.4	0.7	0.3	0.2	0.2	0.0	0.0	0.0	0.0
Select red oaks	7.8	2.1	1.8	1.4	0.9	0.6	0.4	0.3	0.0	0.1	0.0	0.0	0.0	0.0
Other white oaks	68.2	25.0	19.3	10.6	6.1	3.6	2.2	0.8	0.2	0.4	0.0	0.0	0.0	0.0
Other red oaks	40.4	10.0	9.6	6.3	5.0	3.5	2.0	1.4	1.0	1.1	0.3	0.1	0.1	0.0
Hickory	29.0	11.8	7.7	3.7	2.3	1.7	0.8	0.7	0.0	0.2	0.0	0.0	0.0	0.0
Hard maple	0.2	0.1	0.0	0.1	0.0	0.0	0.0	0.0	0.0	0.0	0.0	0.0	0.0	0.0
Soft maple	2.0	0.8	0.4	0.1	0.0	0.1	0.1	0.1	0.0	0.1	0.0	0.1	0.0	0.0
Sweetgum	8.5	4.1	1.7	1.2	0.6	0.5	0.1	0.1	0.1	0.0	0.0	0.0	0.0	0.0
Tupelo and blackgum	2.3	0.8	0.7	0.3	0.2	0.2	0.0	0.0	0.1	0.0	0.0	0.0	0.0	0.0
Ash	7.7	2.5	1.9	1.5	0.9	0.4	0.2	0.1	0.1	0.1	0.0	0.0	0.0	0.0
Cottonwood and aspen	0.9	0.1	0.1	0.1	0.2	0.1	0.1	0.2	0.0	0.0	0.0	0.0	0.0	0.0
Basswood	0.0	0.0	0.0	0.0	0.0	0.0	0.0	0.0	0.0	0.0	0.0	0.0	0.0	0.0
Black walnut	1.0	0.3	0.3	0.1	0.1	0.2	0.1	0.0	0.0	0.0	0.0	0.0	0.0	0.0
Other eastern soft hardwoods	20.2	8.3	5.1	2.8	1.9	0.8	0.4	0.3	0.4	0.1	0.0	0.1	0.0	0.0
Other eastern hard hardwoods	2.5	0.9	0.8	0.4	0.3	0.1	0.0	0.0	0.0	0.0	0.0	0.0	0.0	0.0
Total hardwoods	211.8	74.1	54.5	32.6	20.5	13.1	7.1	4.3	2.2	2.3	0.4	0.4	0.2	0.0
All species	370.2	126.7	94.2	58.3	41.3	25.2	11.9	6.3	2.8	2.5	0.4	0.4	0.2	0.0

Numbers in rows and columns may not sum to totals due to rounding.
0.0 = no sample for the cell or a value of > 0.0 but < 0.05.
[a] Palm species have been included (species codes 906 to 915).

Table A.12—Net[a] volume of live trees on forest land by ownership class and land status, east Oklahoma, 2008

Ownership class	All forest land	Unreserved			Reserved		
		Total	Timberland	Unproductive	Total	Productive	Unproductive
				million cubic feet			
U.S. Forest Service							
National forest	523.6	472.6	467.5	5.0	51.1	51.1	0.0
Total	523.6	472.6	467.5	5.0	51.1	51.1	0.0
Other Federal							
U.S. Fish and Wildlife Service	18.7	18.7	18.7	0.0	0.0	0.0	0.0
Dept. of Defense/Dept. of Energy	305.7	305.7	292.5	13.3	0.0	0.0	0.0
Other Federal	70.9	70.9	70.9	0.0	0.0	0.0	0.0
Total	395.3	395.3	382.1	13.3	0.0	0.0	0.0
State and local government							
State	220.4	169.6	164.3	5.3	50.9	50.9	0.0
Local	31.0	31.0	27.1	3.8	0.0	0.0	0.0
Total	251.4	200.5	191.4	9.1	50.9	50.9	0.0
Forest industry							
Corporate	558.9	558.9	558.9	0.0	0.0	0.0	0.0
Total	558.9	558.9	558.9	0.0	0.0	0.0	0.0
Nonindustrial private							
Corporate	760.5	760.5	724.5	36.0	0.0	0.0	0.0
Conservation/natural resources organization	12.5	12.5	12.5	0.0	0.0	0.0	0.0
Unincorporated partnership/association/club	144.5	144.5	129.9	14.5	0.0	0.0	0.0
Native American	56.2	56.2	56.2	0.0	0.0	0.0	0.0
Individual	2,849.2	2,849.2	2,620.3	228.9	0.0	0.0	0.0
Total	3,822.9	3,822.9	3,543.5	279.4	0.0	0.0	0.0
All classes	5,552.2	5,450.2	5,143.4	306.8	102.0	102.0	0.0

Numbers in rows and columns may not sum to totals due to rounding.
0.0 = no sample for the cell or a value of > 0.0 but < 0.05.
[a] Excludes rotten, missing, and form cull defects volume.

Table A.13—Net[a] volume of live trees on forest land by forest-type group and stand-size class, east Oklahoma, 2008

| Forest-type group[b] | All size classes | Stand-size class | | | |
		Large diameter	Medium diameter	Small diameter	Non-stocked
		million cubic feet			
Softwood					
Loblolly-shortleaf pine	1,367.4	1,117.3	233.3	16.8	0.0
Other eastern softwoods	26.9	7.0	15.4	4.5	0.0
Pinyon-juniper	0.3	0.0	0.3	0.0	0.0
Total softwoods	1,394.6	1,124.3	249.0	21.3	0.0
Hardwood					
Oak-pine	626.0	376.8	227.4	21.7	0.0
Oak-hickory	2,834.3	1,615.3	1,103.8	115.2	0.0
Oak-gum-cypress	205.5	163.3	36.9	5.3	0.0
Elm-ash-cottonwood	489.0	396.8	83.8	8.4	0.0
Other hardwoods	2.2	0.0	2.1	0.1	0.0
Total hardwoods	4,157.0	2,552.3	1,454.0	150.7	0.0
Nonstocked	0.6	0.0	0.0	0.0	0.6
All groups	5,552.2	3,676.6	1,702.9	172.0	0.6

Numbers in rows and columns may not sum to totals due to rounding.

0.0 = no sample for the cell or a value of > 0.0 but < 0.05.

[a] Excludes rotten, missing, and form cull defects volume.

[b] Palm species have been included (species codes 906 to 915).

Table A.13.1—Net[a] volume of live trees on timberland by forest-type group and stand-size class, east Oklahoma, 2008

Forest-type group[b]	All size classes	Stand-size class			
		Large diameter	Medium diameter	Small diameter	Non-stocked
		million cubic feet			
Softwood					
Loblolly-shortleaf pine	1,306.5	1,056.4	233.3	16.8	0.0
Other eastern softwoods	24.7	7.0	13.3	4.5	0.0
Total softwoods	1,331.3	1,063.4	246.5	21.3	0.0
Hardwood					
Oak-pine	578.0	376.8	182.4	18.8	0.0
Oak-hickory	2,536.8	1,520.6	909.9	106.3	0.0
Oak-gum-cypress	205.5	163.3	36.9	5.3	0.0
Elm-ash-cottonwood	489.0	396.8	83.8	8.4	0.0
Other hardwoods	2.2	0.0	2.1	0.1	0.0
Total hardwoods	3,811.5	2,457.5	1,215.1	138.9	0.0
Nonstocked	0.6	0.0	0.0	0.0	0.6
All groups	5,143.4	3,520.9	1,461.6	160.2	0.6

Numbers in rows and columns may not sum to totals due to rounding.

0.0 = no sample for the cell or a value of > 0.0 but < 0.05.

[a] Excludes rotten, missing, and form cull defects volume.

[b] Palm species have been included (species codes 906 to 915).

Table A.14—Net[a] volume of live trees on forest land by species group and ownership group, east Oklahoma, 2008

Species group[b]	All ownerships	U.S. Forest Service	Other Federal	State and local government	Forest industry	Nonindustrial private
				million cubic feet		
Softwood						
Loblolly and shortleaf pines	1,630.8	359.2	71.1	81.3	359.9	759.3
Cypress	0.0	0.0	0.0	0.0	0.0	0.0
Other eastern softwoods	89.9	3.6	5.5	4.1	0.9	75.9
Total softwoods	1,720.7	362.8	76.6	85.4	360.8	835.2
Hardwood						
Select white oaks	331.1	35.3	10.3	22.5	52.7	210.3
Select red oaks	173.4	17.0	28.4	6.3	18.2	103.5
Other white oaks	1,086.3	43.2	77.0	49.6	20.8	895.6
Other red oaks	854.8	20.8	69.0	28.3	35.9	700.8
Hickory	433.7	23.2	36.3	20.5	27.3	326.5
Hard maple	6.6	0.0	0.6	0.5	0.4	5.1
Soft maple	76.4	3.1	1.6	16.6	9.5	45.5
Beech	0.0	0.0	0.0	0.0	0.0	0.0
Sweetgum	93.5	4.7	17.1	0.0	9.1	62.6
Tupelo and blackgum	41.1	5.9	0.3	0.1	2.4	32.4
Ash	176.8	2.5	24.7	7.5	8.4	133.7
Cottonwood and aspen	27.8	0.0	8.8	2.6	0.0	16.5
Basswood	0.7	0.1	0.2	0.0	0.0	0.5
Black walnut	20.2	0.0	1.0	0.8	0.0	18.4
Other eastern soft hardwoods	412.4	4.7	37.4	8.0	12.9	349.3
Other eastern hard hardwoods	45.3	0.1	3.0	2.6	0.2	39.4
Eastern noncommercial hardwoods	50.5	0.2	3.2	0.1	0.3	46.7
Western woodland hardwoods	1.0	0.0	0.0	0.0	0.0	1.0
Total hardwoods	3,831.5	160.9	318.7	166.0	198.1	2,987.7
All species	5,552.2	523.6	395.3	251.4	558.9	3,822.9

Numbers in rows and columns may not sum to totals due to rounding.

0.0 = no sample for the cell or a value of > 0.0 but < 0.05.

[a] Excludes rotten, missing, and form cull defects volume.

[b] Palm species have been included (species codes 906 to 915).

Table A.14.1—Net[a] volume of live trees on timberland by species group and ownership group, east Oklahoma, 2008

Species group[b]	All ownerships	Ownership group				
		U.S. Forest Service	Other Federal	State and local government	Forest industry	Nonindustrial private
		million cubic feet				
Softwood						
Loblolly and shortleaf pines	1,564.7	329.4	71.1	54.1	359.9	750.1
Cypress	0.0	0.0	0.0	0.0	0.0	0.0
Other eastern softwoods	74.3	1.8	4.8	4.1	0.9	62.7
Total softwoods	1,638.9	331.2	75.9	58.2	360.8	812.8
Hardwood						
Select white oaks	309.2	29.9	10.3	9.9	52.7	206.4
Select red oaks	162.5	9.0	28.4	5.1	18.2	101.8
Other white oaks	893.9	37.1	69.9	42.8	20.8	723.3
Other red oaks	816.2	20.8	65.8	22.3	35.9	671.3
Hickory	399.0	22.2	34.5	17.0	27.3	298.1
Hard maple	6.1	0.0	0.6	0.0	0.4	5.1
Soft maple	75.0	2.5	1.6	16.6	9.5	44.9
Beech	0.0	0.0	0.0	0.0	0.0	0.0
Sweetgum	92.9	4.1	17.1	0.0	9.1	62.6
Tupelo and blackgum	38.7	3.6	0.3	0.0	2.4	32.4
Ash	169.4	2.2	24.5	7.5	8.4	126.8
Cottonwood and aspen	27.8	0.0	8.8	2.6	0.0	16.5
Basswood	0.7	0.1	0.2	0.0	0.0	0.5
Black walnut	19.9	0.0	1.0	0.7	0.0	18.1
Other eastern soft hardwoods	399.4	4.7	37.2	6.1	12.9	338.5
Other eastern hard hardwoods	44.5	0.0	3.0	2.4	0.2	38.9
Eastern noncommercial hardwoods	49.3	0.1	3.1	0.1	0.3	45.7
Total hardwoods	3,504.5	136.3	306.1	133.2	198.1	2,730.7
All species	5,143.4	467.5	382.1	191.4	558.9	3,543.5

Numbers in rows and columns may not sum to totals due to rounding.

0.0 = no sample for the cell or a value of > 0.0 but < 0.05.

[a] Excludes rotten, missing, and form cull defects volume.

[b] Palm species have been included (species codes 906 to 915).

Table A.15—Net[a] volume of live trees on forest land by species group and diameter class, east Oklahoma, 2008

Species group[b]	All classes	Diameter class (inches at breast height)												
		5.0–6.9	7.0–8.9	9.0–10.9	11.0–12.9	13.0–14.9	15.0–16.9	17.0–18.9	19.0–20.9	21.0–24.9	25.0–28.9	29.0–32.9	33.0–36.9	37.0+
						million cubic feet								
Softwood														
Loblolly and shortleaf pines	1,630.8	109.8	201.1	277.1	361.6	322.7	189.2	99.1	39.2	24.3	0.0	6.7	0.0	0.0
Cypress	0.0	0.0	0.0	0.0	0.0	0.0	0.0	0.0	0.0	0.0	0.0	0.0	0.0	0.0
Other eastern softwoods	89.9	24.1	23.6	20.6	9.5	6.9	3.2	2.0	0.0	0.0	0.0	0.0	0.0	0.0
Total softwoods	1,720.7	133.9	224.7	297.7	371.1	329.5	192.4	101.2	39.2	24.3	0.0	6.7	0.0	0.0
Hardwood														
Select white oaks	331.1	26.4	41.2	59.2	47.2	46.1	39.6	28.4	10.6	25.7	3.8	3.1	0.0	0.0
Select red oaks	173.4	10.5	18.2	23.9	19.0	23.1	19.5	15.6	3.9	12.8	2.5	6.0	6.7	11.9
Other white oaks	1,086.3	131.8	191.1	176.4	159.8	143.8	117.8	69.4	28.2	39.3	15.5	4.0	9.3	0.0
Other red oaks	854.8	54.2	82.6	99.0	114.5	107.5	81.0	80.6	65.2	85.7	39.4	24.3	20.6	0.0
Hickory	433.7	51.0	67.1	66.4	64.1	60.9	38.5	37.5	8.0	26.6	7.7	5.8	0.0	0.0
Hard maple	6.6	1.5	0.8	1.9	1.9	0.4	0.0	0.0	0.0	0.0	0.0	0.0	0.0	0.0
Soft maple	76.4	7.8	5.9	5.4	2.3	4.7	3.0	11.0	2.1	13.4	6.2	14.7	0.0	0.0
Beech	0.0	0.0	0.0	0.0	0.0	0.0	0.0	0.0	0.0	0.0	0.0	0.0	0.0	0.0
Sweetgum	93.5	13.6	13.6	15.0	14.2	13.9	6.0	8.4	6.7	2.0	0.0	0.0	0.0	0.0
Tupelo and blackgum	41.1	4.2	7.8	5.6	7.1	5.7	3.1	3.3	4.3	0.0	0.0	0.0	0.0	0.0
Ash	176.8	15.9	25.6	27.7	26.2	22.6	13.8	8.6	11.8	14.3	2.6	7.7	0.0	0.0
Cottonwood and aspen	27.8	0.5	1.2	2.6	5.6	2.5	3.1	9.7	2.6	0.0	0.0	0.0	0.0	0.0
Basswood	0.7	0.1	0.2	0.0	0.4	0.0	0.0	0.0	0.0	0.0	0.0	0.0	0.0	0.0
Black walnut	20.2	1.8	3.0	2.9	3.6	4.0	2.9	0.0	0.0	2.0	0.0	0.0	0.0	0.0
Other eastern soft hardwoods	412.4	68.7	70.8	60.6	53.4	33.3	32.8	20.7	22.6	16.7	6.6	16.5	9.7	0.0
Other eastern hard hardwoods	45.3	10.6	11.1	8.5	5.1	5.1	0.0	1.0	0.0	0.9	2.9	0.0	0.0	0.0
Eastern noncommercial hardwoods	50.5	11.0	10.9	8.0	7.4	3.3	1.7	1.0	1.0	2.8	3.3	0.0	0.0	0.0
Western woodland hardwoods	1.0	0.0	0.1	0.4	0.6	0.0	0.0	0.0	0.0	0.0	0.0	0.0	0.0	0.0
Total hardwoods	3,831.5	409.7	551.1	563.4	532.5	476.8	362.8	295.2	166.9	242.3	90.5	82.0	46.3	11.9
All species	5,552.2	543.6	775.9	861.0	903.6	806.4	555.3	396.4	206.1	266.5	90.5	88.7	46.3	11.9

Numbers in rows and columns may not sum to totals due to rounding.

0.0 = no sample for the cell or a value of > 0.0 but < 0.05.

[a] Excludes rotten, missing, and form cull defects volume.

[b] Palm species have been included (species codes 906 to 915).

Table A.15.1—Net[a] volume of live trees on timberland by species group and diameter class, east Oklahoma, 2008

Species group[b]	All classes	Diameter class (inches at breast height)												
		5.0– 6.9	7.0– 8.9	9.0– 10.9	11.0– 12.9	13.0– 14.9	15.0– 16.9	17.0– 18.9	19.0– 20.9	21.0– 24.9	25.0– 28.9	29.0– 32.9	33.0– 36.9	37.0+
		million cubic feet												
Softwood														
Loblolly and shortleaf pines	1,564.7	108.1	197.6	267.5	354.7	308.2	176.6	91.0	36.9	17.4	0.0	6.7	0.0	0.0
Cypress	0.0	0.0	0.0	0.0	0.0	0.0	0.0	0.0	0.0	0.0	0.0	0.0	0.0	0.0
Other eastern softwoods	74.3	19.8	19.9	16.7	7.8	4.9	3.2	2.0	0.0	0.0	0.0	0.0	0.0	0.0
Total softwoods	1,638.9	127.9	217.4	284.2	362.5	313.1	179.8	93.0	36.9	17.4	0.0	6.7	0.0	0.0
Hardwood														
Select white oaks	309.2	24.6	38.7	54.9	42.6	42.8	37.5	27.5	10.6	23.2	3.8	3.1	0.0	0.0
Select red oaks	162.5	10.1	17.4	20.4	17.6	20.0	18.4	14.7	3.9	12.8	2.5	6.0	6.7	11.9
Other white oaks	893.9	96.7	147.9	144.5	136.9	118.2	101.3	57.4	25.5	38.6	13.6	4.0	9.3	0.0
Other red oaks	816.2	47.7	76.0	90.7	107.5	102.3	79.8	80.6	65.2	82.1	39.4	24.3	20.6	0.0
Hickory	399.0	43.5	58.6	59.2	59.4	56.2	36.5	37.5	8.0	26.6	7.7	5.8	0.0	0.0
Hard maple	6.1	1.5	0.7	1.9	1.6	0.4	0.0	0.0	0.0	0.0	0.0	0.0	0.0	0.0
Soft maple	75.0	7.5	5.7	5.0	1.8	4.7	3.0	11.0	2.1	13.4	6.2	14.7	0.0	0.0
Beech	0.0	0.0	0.0	0.0	0.0	0.0	0.0	0.0	0.0	0.0	0.0	0.0	0.0	0.0
Sweetgum	92.9	13.6	13.6	15.0	13.6	13.9	6.0	8.4	6.7	2.0	0.0	0.0	0.0	0.0
Tupelo and blackgum	38.7	3.7	6.9	5.2	6.5	5.7	3.1	3.3	4.3	0.0	0.0	0.0	0.0	0.0
Ash	169.4	15.3	24.9	26.9	24.4	21.7	13.1	8.6	10.0	14.3	2.6	7.7	0.0	0.0
Cottonwood and aspen	27.8	0.5	1.2	2.6	5.6	2.5	3.1	9.7	2.6	0.0	0.0	0.0	0.0	0.0
Basswood	0.7	0.1	0.2	0.0	0.4	0.0	0.0	0.0	0.0	0.0	0.0	0.0	0.0	0.0
Black walnut	19.9	1.7	3.0	2.6	3.6	4.0	2.9	0.0	0.0	2.0	0.0	0.0	0.0	0.0
Other eastern soft hardwoods	399.4	63.8	66.8	58.0	51.9	33.3	32.8	20.7	22.6	16.7	6.6	16.5	9.7	0.0
Other eastern hard hardwoods	44.5	10.2	10.8	8.5	5.1	5.1	0.0	1.0	0.0	0.9	2.9	0.0	0.0	0.0
Eastern noncommercial hardwoods	49.3	10.7	10.7	7.8	7.4	2.9	1.7	1.0	1.0	2.8	3.3	0.0	0.0	0.0
Total hardwoods	3,504.5	351.3	483.1	503.0	486.1	433.6	339.1	281.5	162.4	235.4	88.7	82.0	46.3	11.9
All species	5,143.4	479.2	700.5	787.2	848.6	746.7	518.9	374.5	199.4	252.8	88.7	88.7	46.3	11.9

Numbers in rows and columns may not sum to totals due to rounding.

0.0 = no sample for the cell or a value of > 0.0 but < 0.05.

[a] Excludes rotten, missing, and form cull defects volume.

[b] Palm species have been included (species codes 906 to 915).

Table A.16—Net[a] volume of live trees on forest land by forest-type group and stand origin, east Oklahoma, 2008

| Forest-type group[b] | Total | Stand origin | |
		Natural stands	Artificial regeneration
		million cubic feet	
Softwood			
Loblolly-shortleaf pine	1,367.4	738.2	629.3
Other eastern softwoods	26.9	26.9	0.0
Pinyon-juniper	0.3	0.3	0.0
Total softwoods	1,394.6	765.3	629.3
Hardwood			
Oak-pine	626.0	622.1	3.8
Oak-hickory	2,834.3	2,834.2	0.1
Oak-gum-cypress	205.5	205.5	0.0
Elm-ash-cottonwood	489.0	488.9	0.1
Other hardwoods	2.2	2.2	0.0
Total hardwoods	4,157.0	4,153.0	4.0
Nonstocked	0.6	0.6	0.0
All groups	5,552.2	4,918.9	633.3

Numbers in rows and columns may not sum to totals due to rounding.

0.0 = no sample for the cell or a value of > 0.0 but < 0.05.

[a] Excludes rotten, missing, and form cull defects volume.

[b] Palm species have been included (species codes 906 to 915).

Table A.16.1—Net[a] volume of live trees on timberland by forest-type group and stand origin, east Oklahoma, 2008

| | | Stand origin | |
Forest-type group[b]	Total	Natural stands	Artificial regeneration
		million cubic feet	
Softwood			
Loblolly-shortleaf pine	1,306.5	677.3	629.3
Other eastern softwoods	24.7	24.7	0.0
Total softwoods	1,331.3	702.0	629.3
Hardwood			
Oak-pine	578.0	575.2	2.8
Oak-hickory	2,536.8	2,536.8	0.1
Oak-gum-cypress	205.5	205.5	0.0
Elm-ash-cottonwood	489.0	488.9	0.1
Other hardwoods	2.2	2.2	0.0
Total hardwoods	3,811.5	3,808.5	2.9
Nonstocked	0.6	0.6	0.0
All groups	5,143.4	4,511.2	632.2

Numbers in rows and columns may not sum to totals due to rounding.
0.0 = no sample for the cell or a value of > 0.0 but < 0.05.
[a] Excludes rotten, missing, and form cull defects volume.
[b] Palm species have been included (species codes 906 to 915).

Table A.17—Net[a] volume of growing-stock trees on timberland by species group and diameter class, east Oklahoma, 2008

Species group[b]	All classes	Diameter class *(inches at breast height)*												
		5.0– 6.9	7.0– 8.9	9.0– 10.9	11.0– 12.9	13.0– 14.9	15.0– 16.9	17.0– 18.9	19.0– 20.9	21.0– 24.9	25.0– 28.9	29.0– 32.9	33.0– 36.9	37.0+
						million cubic feet								
Softwood														
Loblolly and shortleaf pines	1,476.6	96.8	182.4	256.2	341.4	291.9	165.8	87.0	34.9	13.5	0.0	6.7	0.0	0.0
Cypress	0.0	0.0	0.0	0.0	0.0	0.0	0.0	0.0	0.0	0.0	0.0	0.0	0.0	0.0
Other eastern softwoods	33.5	9.7	10.4	8.1	3.2	2.0	0.0	0.0	0.0	0.0	0.0	0.0	0.0	0.0
Total softwoods	1,510.1	106.5	192.8	264.4	344.6	293.9	165.8	87.0	34.9	13.5	0.0	6.7	0.0	0.0
Hardwood														
Select white oaks	212.9	18.8	30.2	43.4	31.3	32.1	27.3	12.1	7.9	10.0	0.0	0.0	0.0	0.0
Select red oaks	127.5	6.2	11.3	15.2	14.6	13.2	14.4	13.7	2.4	9.5	2.5	6.0	6.7	11.9
Other white oaks	520.5	55.9	95.5	91.6	83.6	69.3	58.5	25.7	10.0	20.5	3.1	0.0	6.8	0.0
Other red oaks	582.7	23.8	51.5	60.0	76.3	75.1	59.8	55.8	48.9	76.8	26.4	13.8	14.5	0.0
Hickory	252.4	24.0	36.9	35.1	35.2	40.8	24.6	30.6	1.8	17.5	0.0	5.8	0.0	0.0
Hard maple	1.6	0.1	0.0	1.1	0.4	0.0	0.0	0.0	0.0	0.0	0.0	0.0	0.0	0.0
Soft maple	54.5	2.1	2.6	1.7	0.6	2.2	3.0	7.3	2.1	12.0	6.2	14.7	0.0	0.0
Sweetgum	74.2	9.9	10.8	12.5	10.4	13.9	4.6	5.6	4.4	2.0	0.0	0.0	0.0	0.0
Tupelo and blackgum	23.1	1.9	3.9	2.8	3.0	3.9	1.1	2.1	4.3	0.0	0.0	0.0	0.0	0.0
Ash	89.9	6.0	11.5	16.0	13.3	9.7	5.5	6.1	5.4	8.8	0.0	7.7	0.0	0.0
Cottonwood and aspen	24.8	0.3	0.4	1.6	4.7	2.5	3.1	9.7	2.6	0.0	0.0	0.0	0.0	0.0
Basswood	0.2	0.0	0.2	0.0	0.0	0.0	0.0	0.0	0.0	0.0	0.0	0.0	0.0	0.0
Black walnut	10.9	0.7	1.2	1.2	2.1	3.4	2.3	0.0	0.0	0.0	0.0	0.0	0.0	0.0
Other eastern soft hardwoods	193.5	19.4	26.5	25.6	28.1	17.7	12.8	14.5	18.6	5.4	3.6	11.6	9.7	0.0
Other eastern hard hardwoods	20.0	2.2	3.9	4.3	3.6	3.0	0.0	0.0	0.0	0.0	2.9	0.0	0.0	0.0
Total hardwoods	2,188.7	171.4	286.3	312.1	307.1	286.8	217.0	183.1	108.4	162.6	44.8	59.6	37.7	11.9
All species	3,698.8	278.0	479.1	576.5	651.7	580.7	382.8	270.1	143.3	176.0	44.8	66.3	37.7	11.9

Numbers in rows and columns may not sum to totals due to rounding.

0.0 = no sample for the cell or a value of > 0.0 but < 0.05.

[a] Excludes rotten, missing, and form cull defects volume.

[b] Palm species have been included (species codes 906 to 915).

Table A.18—Net[a] volume of growing-stock trees on timberland by species group and ownership group, east Oklahoma, 2008

Species group[b]	All ownerships	U.S. Forest Service	Other Federal	State and local government	Forest industry	Nonindustrial private
				million cubic feet		
Softwood						
Loblolly and shortleaf pines	1,476.6	319.4	68.9	48.9	345.9	693.5
Cypress	0.0	0.0	0.0	0.0	0.0	0.0
Other eastern softwoods	33.5	1.4	3.4	1.0	0.3	27.4
Total softwoods	1,510.1	320.8	72.4	49.9	346.2	720.9
Hardwood						
Select white oaks	212.9	21.8	4.0	7.0	32.4	147.7
Select red oaks	127.5	7.0	28.1	2.9	16.2	73.4
Other white oaks	520.5	22.2	50.0	25.3	18.4	404.6
Other red oaks	582.7	14.8	50.5	13.5	28.6	475.3
Hickory	252.4	17.5	25.2	10.2	20.7	178.8
Hard maple	1.6	0.0	0.3	0.0	0.0	1.3
Soft maple	54.5	0.5	0.5	14.5	6.2	32.9
Sweetgum	74.2	3.7	16.4	0.0	7.3	46.8
Tupelo and blackgum	23.1	1.7	0.3	0.0	1.0	20.1
Ash	89.9	0.0	16.1	4.8	6.8	62.2
Cottonwood and aspen	24.8	0.0	8.8	2.6	0.0	13.5
Basswood	0.2	0.0	0.2	0.0	0.0	0.0
Black walnut	10.9	0.0	0.5	0.7	0.0	9.7
Other eastern soft hardwoods	193.5	2.7	21.6	1.7	4.9	162.6
Other eastern hard hardwoods	20.0	0.0	0.8	1.4	0.0	17.8
Total hardwoods	2,188.7	91.9	223.3	84.4	142.6	1,646.5
All species	3,698.8	412.6	295.7	134.3	488.7	2,367.4

Numbers in rows and columns may not sum to totals due to rounding.

0.0 = no sample for the cell or a value of > 0.0 but < 0.05.

[a] Excludes rotten, missing, and form cull defects volume.

[b] Palm species have been included (species codes 906 to 915).

Table A.19—Net[a] volume of sawtimber trees on timberland by species group and diameter class, east Oklahoma, 2008

Species group[b]	All classes	Diameter class (inches at breast height)										
		9.0–10.9	11.0–12.9	13.0–14.9	15.0–16.9	17.0–18.9	19.0–20.9	21.0–24.9	25.0–28.9	29.0–32.9	33.0–36.9	37.0+
		million board feet[c]										
Softwood												
Loblolly and shortleaf pines	5,804.9	950.5	1,549.7	1,501.4	933.2	517.4	217.8	87.7	0.0	47.2	0.0	0.0
Cypress	0.0	0.0	0.0	0.0	0.0	0.0	0.0	0.0	0.0	0.0	0.0	0.0
Other eastern softwoods	59.2	33.3	15.4	10.5	0.0	0.0	0.0	0.0	0.0	0.0	0.0	0.0
Total softwoods	5,864.1	983.8	1,565.1	1,511.9	933.2	517.4	217.8	87.7	0.0	47.2	0.0	0.0
Hardwood												
Select white oaks	504.0	0.0	105.0	127.8	121.6	56.8	39.3	53.5	0.0	0.0	0.0	0.0
Select red oaks	454.1	0.0	49.1	51.3	62.7	65.3	12.0	51.0	13.0	34.8	40.4	74.6
Other white oaks	1,232.8	0.0	306.2	294.3	275.2	128.2	53.0	114.1	18.1	0.0	43.8	0.0
Other red oaks	2,081.8	0.0	264.9	299.6	267.2	266.6	245.8	413.7	150.4	83.2	90.6	0.0
Hickory	689.9	0.0	121.4	165.8	110.6	150.7	9.2	97.0	0.0	35.2	0.0	0.0
Hard maple	1.5	0.0	1.5	0.0	0.0	0.0	0.0	0.0	0.0	0.0	0.0	0.0
Soft maple	270.7	0.0	1.7	9.2	13.6	36.6	11.1	67.8	38.2	92.4	0.0	0.0
Sweetgum	183.7	0.0	37.6	59.3	21.8	28.7	24.6	11.7	0.0	0.0	0.0	0.0
Tupelo and blackgum	59.5	0.0	9.2	14.7	4.6	9.7	21.3	0.0	0.0	0.0	0.0	0.0
Ash	252.1	0.0	43.5	37.9	23.2	28.7	26.2	47.2	0.0	45.4	0.0	0.0
Cottonwood and aspen	103.8	0.0	16.8	10.3	14.3	48.5	13.8	0.0	0.0	0.0	0.0	0.0
Basswood	0.0	0.0	0.0	0.0	0.0	0.0	0.0	0.0	0.0	0.0	0.0	0.0
Black walnut	28.2	0.0	7.1	12.2	9.0	0.0	0.0	0.0	0.0	0.0	0.0	0.0
Other eastern soft hardwoods	558.8	0.0	94.6	69.7	56.5	69.5	91.5	29.8	20.4	67.6	59.3	0.0
Other eastern hard hardwoods	40.1	0.0	12.4	12.0	0.0	0.0	0.0	0.0	15.6	0.0	0.0	0.0
Total hardwoods	6,461.0	0.0	1,070.9	1,164.2	980.1	889.2	547.8	885.9	255.6	358.6	234.0	74.6
All species	12,325.1	983.8	2,636.0	2,676.1	1,913.3	1,406.6	765.6	973.6	255.6	405.8	234.0	74.6

Numbers in rows and columns may not sum to totals due to rounding.

0.0 = no sample for the cell or a value of > 0.0 but < 0.05.

[a] Excludes rotten, missing, and form cull defects volume.

[b] Palm species have been included (species codes 906 to 915).

[c] International ¼-inch rule.

Table A.20—Net[a] volume of sawtimber trees on timberland by species group and ownership group, east Oklahoma, 2008

		Ownership group				
Species group[b]	All ownerships	U.S. Forest Service	Other Federal	State and local government	Forest industry	Nonindustrial private
				million board feet[c]		
Softwood						
Loblolly and shortleaf pines	5,804.9	1,284.0	300.8	234.2	1,307.1	2,678.9
Cypress	0.0	0.0	0.0	0.0	0.0	0.0
Other eastern softwoods	59.2	1.5	7.1	3.2	0.0	47.4
Total softwoods	5,864.1	1,285.5	307.9	237.3	1,307.1	2,726.3
Hardwood						
Select white oaks	504.0	69.3	11.9	16.2	78.6	327.9
Select red oaks	454.1	16.7	134.6	8.9	67.2	226.8
Other white oaks	1,232.8	39.9	123.5	60.9	60.6	947.9
Other red oaks	2,081.8	61.1	187.9	41.8	83.3	1,707.7
Hickory	689.9	44.7	73.1	20.9	45.1	506.1
Hard maple	1.5	0.0	0.0	0.0	0.0	1.5
Soft maple	270.7	0.0	0.0	90.1	27.1	153.5
Sweetgum	183.7	4.5	30.8	0.0	15.3	133.1
Tupelo and blackgum	59.5	3.0	0.0	0.0	0.0	56.5
Ash	252.1	0.0	48.4	20.3	21.5	161.9
Cottonwood and aspen	103.8	0.0	36.7	13.8	0.0	53.3
Basswood	0.0	0.0	0.0	0.0	0.0	0.0
Black walnut	28.2	0.0	0.0	1.9	0.0	26.4
Other eastern soft hardwoods	558.8	2.7	66.9	3.1	5.5	480.6
Other eastern hard hardwoods	40.1	0.0	1.4	4.0	0.0	34.7
Total hardwoods	6,461.0	241.9	715.3	281.9	404.1	4,817.7
All species	12,325.1	1,527.4	1,023.2	519.2	1,711.2	7,544.1

Numbers in rows and columns may not sum to totals due to rounding.

0.0 = no sample for the cell or a value of > 0.0 but < 0.05.

[a] Excludes rotten, missing, and form cull defects volume.

[b] Palm species have been included (species codes 906 to 915).

[c] International ¼-inch rule.

Table A.21—Aboveground dry weight of live trees on forest land by ownership class and land status, east Oklahoma, 2008

Ownership class	All forest land	Unreserved			Reserved		
		Total	Timberland	Unpro-ductive	Total	Pro-ductive	Unpro-ductive
		thousand tons					
U.S. Forest Service							
National forest	13,650.8	12,361.8	12,202.3	159.5	1,289.0	1,289.0	0.0
Total	13,650.8	12,361.8	12,202.3	159.5	1,289.0	1,289.0	0.0
Other Federal							
U.S. Fish and Wildlife Service	552.0	552.0	552.0	0.0	0.0	0.0	0.0
Dept. of Defense/Dept. of Energy	8,637.5	8,637.5	8,192.6	444.9	0.0	0.0	0.0
Other Federal	1,994.7	1,994.7	1,994.7	0.0	0.0	0.0	0.0
Total	11,184.3	11,184.3	10,739.3	444.9	0.0	0.0	0.0
State and local government							
State	6,346.6	4,987.8	4,764.9	223.0	1,358.7	1,358.7	0.0
Local	970.6	970.6	829.7	140.9	0.0	0.0	0.0
Total	7,317.2	5,958.4	5,594.6	363.8	1,358.7	1,358.7	0.0
Forest industry							
Corporate	15,217.6	15,217.6	15,217.6	0.0	0.0	0.0	0.0
Total	15,217.6	15,217.6	15,217.6	0.0	0.0	0.0	0.0
Nonindustrial private							
Corporate	22,086.7	22,086.7	20,902.9	1,183.8	0.0	0.0	0.0
Conservation/natural resources organization	392.2	392.2	392.2	0.0	0.0	0.0	0.0
Unincorporated partnership/ association/club	4,227.2	4,227.2	3,717.8	509.4	0.0	0.0	0.0
Native American	1,776.7	1,776.7	1,776.7	0.0	0.0	0.0	0.0
Individual	86,677.5	86,677.5	78,780.5	7,897.0	0.0	0.0	0.0
Total	115,160.3	115,160.3	105,570.1	9,590.2	0.0	0.0	0.0
All classes	162,530.1	159,882.4	149,323.9	10,558.5	2,647.7	2,647.7	0.0

Numbers in rows and columns may not sum to totals due to rounding.
0.0 = no sample for the cell or a value of >0.0 but <0.05.

Table A.21.1—Aboveground green weight of live trees on forest land by ownership class and land status, east Oklahoma, 2008

Ownership class	All forest land	Unreserved			Reserved		
		Total	Timberland	Unpro-ductive	Total	Productive	Unpro-ductive
			thousand tons				
U.S. Forest Service							
National forest	27,301.7	24,723.7	24,404.6	319.1	2,578.0	2,578.0	0.0
Total	27,301.7	24,723.7	24,404.6	319.1	2,578.0	2,578.0	0.0
Other Federal							
U.S. Fish and Wildlife Service	1,104.1	1,104.1	1,104.1	0.0	0.0	0.0	0.0
Dept. of Defense/Dept. of Energy	17,275.1	17,275.1	16,385.2	889.9	0.0	0.0	0.0
Other Federal	3,989.4	3,989.4	3,989.4	0.0	0.0	0.0	0.0
Total	22,368.5	22,368.5	21,478.6	889.9	0.0	0.0	0.0
State and local government							
State	12,693.1	9,975.7	9,529.7	446.0	2,717.4	2,717.4	0.0
Local	1,941.2	1,941.2	1,659.5	281.7	0.0	0.0	0.0
Total	14,634.3	11,916.9	11,189.2	727.7	2,717.4	2,717.4	0.0
Forest industry							
Corporate	30,435.2	30,435.2	30,435.2	0.0	0.0	0.0	0.0
Total	30,435.2	30,435.2	30,435.2	0.0	0.0	0.0	0.0
Nonindustrial private							
Corporate	44,173.4	44,173.4	41,805.7	2,367.7	0.0	0.0	0.0
Conservation/natural resources organization	784.4	784.4	784.4	0.0	0.0	0.0	0.0
Unincorporated partnership/ association/club	8,454.4	8,454.4	7,435.7	1,018.7	0.0	0.0	0.0
Native American	3,553.5	3,553.5	3,553.5	0.0	0.0	0.0	0.0
Individual	173,354.9	173,354.9	157,560.9	15,794.0	0.0	0.0	0.0
Total	230,320.5	230,320.5	211,140.2	19,180.4	0.0	0.0	0.0
All classes	325,060.3	319,764.9	298,647.9	21,117.0	5,295.4	5,295.4	0.0

Numbers in rows and columns may not sum to totals due to rounding.
0.0 = no sample for the cell or a value of > 0.0 but < 0.05.

Table A.22—Aboveground dry weight of live trees on forest land by species group and diameter class, east Oklahoma, 2008

Species group[a]	All classes	Diameter class (inches at breast height)														
		1.0–2.9	3.0–4.9	5.0–6.9	7.0–8.9	9.0–10.9	11.0–12.9	13.0–14.9	15.0–16.9	17.0–18.9	19.0–20.9	21.0–24.9	25.0–28.9	29.0–32.9	33.0–36.9	37.0+
		thousand tons														
Softwood																
Loblolly and shortleaf pines	38,223.2	495.3	1,573.5	2,742.5	4,589.5	6,084.4	7,884.3	7,001.9	4,131.7	2,177.6	854.4	527.1	0.0	160.9	0.0	0.0
Cypress	0.0	0.0	0.0	0.0	0.0	0.0	0.0	0.0	0.0	0.0	0.0	0.0	0.0	0.0	0.0	0.0
Other eastern softwoods	3,094.9	320.2	460.0	746.6	600.0	479.7	215.1	157.1	70.9	45.4	0.0	0.0	0.0	0.0	0.0	0.0
Total softwoods	41,318.1	815.5	2,033.5	3,489.2	5,189.4	6,564.2	8,099.4	7,159.0	4,202.6	2,223.1	854.4	527.1	0.0	160.9	0.0	0.0
Hardwood																
Select white oaks	9,768.0	147.8	398.3	728.2	1,090.9	1,573.2	1,269.9	1,278.9	1,131.0	818.9	322.5	784.1	109.3	115.1	0.0	0.0
Select red oaks	5,414.0	94.1	267.3	289.6	497.1	639.3	524.2	659.6	554.6	447.8	141.6	419.7	106.9	182.4	216.4	373.2
Other white oaks	34,055.2	724.4	1,750.4	3,840.5	5,265.2	4,857.8	4,500.4	4,186.8	3,538.9	2,137.1	909.9	1,262.4	520.1	153.0	408.6	0.0
Other red oaks	28,920.2	845.7	1,485.8	1,958.8	2,666.3	3,037.4	3,387.2	3,223.2	2,440.4	2,466.3	2,135.8	2,682.1	1,231.2	799.7	560.2	0.0
Hickory	14,111.9	796.2	1,433.7	1,521.0	1,770.0	1,736.8	1,697.5	1,627.5	1,038.7	1,067.1	250.0	783.3	218.5	171.7	0.0	0.0
Hard maple	231.1	19.5	26.1	42.0	21.5	53.2	58.1	10.7	0.0	0.0	0.0	0.0	0.0	0.0	0.0	0.0
Soft maple	2,396.3	233.0	296.8	207.8	153.9	132.9	55.7	113.9	69.4	256.4	47.9	349.0	151.3	328.3	0.0	0.0
Beech	17.9	7.2	10.6	0.0	0.0	0.0	0.0	0.0	0.0	0.0	0.0	0.0	0.0	0.0	0.0	0.0
Sweetgum	2,546.2	126.0	252.3	357.6	307.3	327.9	311.9	308.4	140.3	196.2	173.8	44.6	0.0	0.0	0.0	0.0
Tupelo and blackgum	1,140.5	108.9	157.4	85.0	156.9	116.7	146.4	124.2	70.3	74.9	99.8	0.0	0.0	0.0	0.0	0.0
Ash	4,014.1	157.2	333.5	416.3	566.4	570.0	518.0	426.2	255.5	148.8	214.8	243.8	49.9	113.5	0.0	0.0
Cottonwood and aspen	598.8	0.0	0.0	10.6	25.2	52.5	118.3	53.2	67.5	214.0	57.7	0.0	0.0	0.0	0.0	0.0
Basswood	32.1	8.4	7.9	2.3	3.1	0.0	10.4	0.0	0.0	0.0	0.0	0.0	0.0	0.0	0.0	0.0
Black walnut	681.7	5.2	28.0	51.3	89.9	86.8	113.6	126.7	113.4	0.0	0.0	66.8	0.0	0.0	0.0	0.0
Other eastern soft hardwoods	12,591.7	1,156.7	1,985.5	1,461.9	1,498.1	1,323.6	1,199.9	769.3	763.6	498.3	603.6	445.3	156.1	475.0	254.8	0.0
Other eastern hard hardwoods	2,390.2	480.1	549.5	317.9	314.0	238.5	143.1	149.1	0.0	42.5	0.0	67.2	88.3	0.0	0.0	0.0
Eastern noncommercial hardwoods	2,276.1	478.3	525.8	338.2	268.4	188.0	164.5	72.4	46.7	29.0	21.5	60.6	82.7	0.0	0.0	0.0
Western woodland hardwoods	25.8	0.0	0.0	0.0	2.2	9.6	14.0	0.0	0.0	0.0	0.0	0.0	0.0	0.0	0.0	0.0
Total hardwoods	121,212.1	5,388.8	9,508.9	11,629.0	14,696.4	14,943.8	14,233.1	13,130.0	10,230.3	8,397.5	4,978.9	7,208.9	2,714.4	2,338.7	1,440.1	373.2
All species	162,530.1	6,204.3	11,542.4	15,118.1	19,885.9	21,508.0	22,332.5	20,289.0	14,432.9	10,620.5	5,833.3	7,735.9	2,714.4	2,499.6	1,440.1	373.2

Numbers in rows and columns may not sum to totals due to rounding.

0.0 = no sample for the cell or a value of >0.0 but <0.05.

[a] Palm species have been included (species codes 906 to 915).

Table A.22.1—Aboveground dry weight of live trees on timberland by species group and diameter class, east Oklahoma, 2008

Species group[a]	All classes	Diameter class (inches at breast height)														
		1.0–2.9	3.0–4.9	5.0–6.9	7.0–8.9	9.0–10.9	11.0–12.9	13.0–14.9	15.0–16.9	17.0–18.9	19.0–20.9	21.0–24.9	25.0–28.9	29.0–32.9	33.0–36.9	37.0+
		thousand tons														
Softwood																
Loblolly and shortleaf pines	36,702.1	486.3	1,498.4	2,703.8	4,509.6	5,877.2	7,735.3	6,688.3	3,857.8	2,001.0	806.0	377.6	0.0	160.9	0.0	0.0
Cypress	0.0	0.0	0.0	0.0	0.0	0.0	0.0	0.0	0.0	0.0	0.0	0.0	0.0	0.0	0.0	0.0
Other eastern softwoods	2,496.6	262.1	331.0	608.2	503.2	386.6	176.6	112.9	70.9	45.4	0.0	0.0	0.0	0.0	0.0	0.0
Total softwoods	39,198.7	748.4	1,829.3	3,312.1	5,012.9	6,263.5	7,911.9	6,801.2	3,928.7	2,046.4	806.0	377.6	0.0	160.9	0.0	0.0
Hardwood																
Select white oaks	9,144.3	144.0	379.6	679.5	1,025.2	1,460.8	1,148.4	1,187.9	1,066.8	791.7	322.5	713.7	109.3	115.1	0.0	0.0
Select red oaks	5,108.7	91.1	259.3	277.5	475.2	546.6	489.5	577.2	526.7	425.3	141.6	419.7	106.9	182.4	216.4	373.2
Other white oaks	27,806.7	587.3	1,237.6	2,803.0	4,067.4	3,970.5	3,854.1	3,451.1	3,015.9	1,750.5	822.6	1,233.1	451.7	153.0	408.6	0.0
Other red oaks	27,303.4	757.8	1,341.8	1,677.7	2,409.1	2,737.6	3,150.1	3,060.7	2,400.3	2,466.3	2,135.8	2,575.1	1,231.2	799.7	560.2	0.0
Hickory	12,850.3	697.4	1,241.4	1,286.8	1,544.8	1,544.3	1,567.1	1,500.8	977.2	1,067.1	250.0	783.3	218.5	171.7	0.0	0.0
Hard maple	218.6	19.5	26.1	42.0	18.4	53.2	48.7	10.7	0.0	0.0	0.0	0.0	0.0	0.0	0.0	0.0
Soft maple	2,332.8	227.8	271.4	200.5	149.1	124.4	43.4	113.9	69.4	256.4	47.9	349.0	0.0	328.3	0.0	0.0
Beech	17.9	7.2	10.6	0.0	0.0	0.0	0.0	0.0	0.0	0.0	0.0	0.0	0.0	0.0	0.0	0.0
Sweetgum	2,533.3	126.0	252.3	357.6	307.3	327.9	299.0	308.4	140.3	196.2	173.8	44.6	0.0	0.0	0.0	0.0
Tupelo and blackgum	1,083.3	106.4	150.7	75.7	139.5	108.6	133.3	124.2	70.3	74.9	99.8	0.0	0.0	0.0	0.0	0.0
Ash	3,862.1	155.7	333.5	399.3	548.8	552.5	481.9	408.4	241.4	148.8	184.5	243.8	49.9	113.5	0.0	0.0
Cottonwood and aspen	598.8	0.0	0.0	10.6	25.2	52.5	118.3	53.2	67.5	214.0	57.7	0.0	0.0	0.0	0.0	0.0
Basswood	32.1	8.4	7.9	2.3	3.1	0.0	10.4	0.0	0.0	0.0	0.0	0.0	0.0	0.0	0.0	0.0
Black walnut	672.3	5.2	28.0	49.4	89.9	79.3	113.6	126.7	113.4	0.0	0.0	66.8	0.0	0.0	0.0	0.0
Other eastern soft hardwoods	11,992.6	1,040.8	1,777.4	1,358.6	1,414.6	1,268.6	1,166.6	769.3	763.6	498.3	603.6	445.3	156.1	475.0	254.8	0.0
Other eastern hard hardwoods	2,358.1	471.9	549.5	305.6	302.3	238.5	143.1	149.1	0.0	42.5	0.0	67.2	88.3	0.0	0.0	0.0
Eastern noncommercial hardwoods	2,209.9	453.8	513.5	327.6	263.5	182.6	164.5	63.9	46.7	29.0	21.5	60.6	82.7	0.0	0.0	0.0
Total hardwoods	110,125.2	4,900.3	8,380.6	9,853.6	12,783.4	13,248.0	12,932.0	11,905.4	9,499.5	7,961.1	4,861.3	7,002.1	2,645.9	2,338.7	1,440.1	373.2
All species	149,323.9	5,648.7	10,210.0	13,165.7	17,796.2	19,511.4	20,843.8	18,706.6	13,428.2	10,007.5	5,667.3	7,379.7	2,645.9	2,499.6	1,440.1	373.2

Numbers in rows and columns may not sum to totals due to rounding.

0.0 = no sample for the cell or a value of >0.0 but <0.05.

[a] Palm species have been included (species codes 906 to 915).

Table A.22.2—Aboveground green weight of live trees on forest land by species group and diameter class, east Oklahoma, 2008

Species group[a]	All classes	Diameter class (inches at breast height)														
		1.0–2.9	3.0–4.9	5.0–6.9	7.0–8.9	9.0–10.9	11.0–12.9	13.0–14.9	15.0–16.9	17.0–18.9	19.0–20.9	21.0–24.9	25.0–28.9	29.0–32.9	33.0–36.9	37.0+
								thousand tons								
Softwood																
Loblolly and shortleaf pines	76,446.4	990.6	3,147.0	5,485.1	9,179.0	12,168.9	15,768.7	14,003.8	8,263.4	4,355.3	1,708.7	1,054.2	0.0	321.8	0.0	0.0
Cypress	0.0	0.0	0.0	0.0	0.0	0.0	0.0	0.0	0.0	0.0	0.0	0.0	0.0	0.0	0.0	0.0
Other eastern softwoods	6,189.8	640.3	919.9	1,493.2	1,199.9	959.5	430.1	314.1	141.8	90.8	0.0	0.0	0.0	0.0	0.0	0.0
Total softwoods	82,636.1	1,630.9	4,066.9	6,978.3	10,378.9	13,128.3	16,198.8	14,317.9	8,405.2	4,446.1	1,708.7	1,054.2	0.0	321.8	0.0	0.0
Hardwood																
Select white oaks	19,536.0	295.5	796.7	1,456.4	2,181.8	3,146.4	2,539.4	2,557.8	2,261.9	1,637.9	644.9	1,568.2	218.5	230.1	0.0	0.0
Select red oaks	10,828.0	188.2	534.6	579.2	994.2	1,278.7	1,048.4	1,319.2	1,109.2	895.7	283.2	839.3	213.8	364.9	432.9	746.5
Other white oaks	68,110.5	1,448.8	3,500.8	7,681.0	10,530.5	9,714.6	9,000.8	8,373.6	7,077.8	4,274.3	1,819.9	2,524.8	1,040.3	306.1	817.1	0.0
Other red oaks	57,840.4	1,691.5	2,971.6	3,917.6	5,332.7	6,074.8	6,774.4	6,446.4	4,880.8	4,932.6	4,271.6	5,364.3	2,462.4	1,599.4	1,120.4	0.0
Hickory	28,223.8	1,592.4	2,867.3	3,042.1	3,540.0	3,473.5	3,395.0	3,255.0	2,077.4	2,134.2	499.9	1,566.6	436.9	343.3	0.0	0.0
Hard maple	462.3	39.0	52.2	84.1	43.1	106.5	116.2	21.3	0.0	0.0	0.0	0.0	0.0	0.0	0.0	0.0
Soft maple	4,792.7	466.1	593.6	415.6	307.8	265.8	111.4	227.7	138.7	512.9	95.8	698.0	302.7	656.6	0.0	0.0
Beech	35.7	14.4	21.3	0.0	0.0	0.0	0.0	0.0	0.0	0.0	0.0	0.0	0.0	0.0	0.0	0.0
Sweetgum	5,092.5	251.9	504.5	715.1	614.6	655.8	623.8	616.9	280.6	392.4	347.7	89.2	0.0	0.0	0.0	0.0
Tupelo and blackgum	2,281.0	217.9	314.8	170.0	313.8	233.5	292.8	248.3	140.6	149.8	199.6	0.0	0.0	0.0	0.0	0.0
Ash	8,028.3	314.4	667.1	832.7	1,132.8	1,140.1	1,036.1	852.4	511.0	297.7	429.7	487.6	99.9	227.0	0.0	0.0
Cottonwood and aspen	1,197.7	0.0	0.0	21.2	50.4	105.0	236.6	106.3	135.0	427.9	115.4	0.0	0.0	0.0	0.0	0.0
Basswood	64.3	16.8	15.9	4.6	6.2	0.0	20.8	0.0	0.0	0.0	0.0	0.0	0.0	0.0	0.0	0.0
Black walnut	1,363.3	10.4	56.0	102.7	179.7	173.6	227.1	253.3	226.9	0.0	0.0	133.6	0.0	0.0	0.0	0.0
Other eastern soft hardwoods	25,183.4	2,313.5	3,971.0	2,923.7	2,996.3	2,647.1	2,399.8	1,538.7	1,527.2	996.7	1,207.2	890.6	312.1	950.0	509.6	0.0
Other eastern hard hardwoods	4,780.5	960.1	1,099.0	635.7	628.0	477.1	286.3	298.3	0.0	85.0	134.4	0.0	176.6	0.0	0.0	0.0
Eastern noncommercial hardwoods	4,552.2	956.7	1,051.5	676.4	536.8	376.0	329.0	144.8	93.5	58.1	43.0	121.1	165.4	0.0	0.0	0.0
Western woodland hardwoods	51.6	0.0	0.0	0.0	4.5	19.2	27.9	0.0	0.0	0.0	0.0	0.0	0.0	0.0	0.0	0.0
Total hardwoods	242,424.1	10,777.7	19,017.9	23,257.9	29,392.9	29,887.6	28,466.3	26,260.0	20,460.7	16,795.0	9,957.9	14,417.7	5,428.7	4,677.4	2,880.1	746.5
All species	325,060.3	12,408.6	23,084.8	30,236.2	39,771.8	43,016.0	44,665.1	40,578.0	28,865.8	21,241.1	11,666.6	15,471.9	5,428.7	4,999.1	2,880.1	746.5

Numbers in rows and columns may not sum to totals due to rounding.
0.0 = no sample for the cell or a value of > 0.0 but <0.05.
[a] Palm species have been included (species codes 906 to 915).

Table A.22.3—Aboveground green weight of live trees on timberland by species group and diameter class, east Oklahoma, 2008

Species group[a]	All classes	Diameter class (inches at breast height)														
		1.0–2.9	3.0–4.9	5.0–6.9	7.0–8.9	9.0–10.9	11.0–12.9	13.0–14.9	15.0–16.9	17.0–18.9	19.0–20.9	21.0–24.9	25.0–28.9	29.0–32.9	33.0–36.9	37.0+
		thousand tons														
Softwood																
Loblolly and shortleaf pines	73,404.1	972.6	2,996.7	5,407.7	9,019.2	11,754.5	15,470.5	13,376.6	7,715.6	4,001.9	1,612.0	755.1	0.0	0.0	0.0	0.0
Cypress	0.0	0.0	0.0	0.0	0.0	0.0	0.0	0.0	0.0	0.0	0.0	0.0	0.0	321.8	0.0	0.0
Other eastern softwoods	4,993.3	524.1	662.0	1,216.5	1,006.5	772.5	353.2	225.8	141.8	90.8	0.0	0.0	0.0	0.0	0.0	0.0
Total softwoods	78,397.4	1,496.8	3,658.7	6,624.1	10,025.7	12,527.0	15,823.7	13,602.4	7,857.4	4,092.8	1,612.0	755.1	0.0	321.8	0.0	0.0
Hardwood																
Select white oaks	18,288.6	288.0	759.1	1,359.1	2,050.4	2,921.6	2,296.8	2,375.7	2,133.5	1,583.4	644.9	1,427.4	218.5	230.1	0.0	0.0
Select red oaks	10,217.4	182.2	518.7	554.9	950.5	1,093.2	979.0	1,154.3	1,053.5	850.6	283.2	839.3	213.8	364.9	432.9	746.5
Other white oaks	55,613.4	1,174.7	2,475.2	5,606.0	8,134.9	7,941.0	7,708.3	6,902.3	6,031.8	3,501.0	1,645.3	2,466.2	903.4	306.1	817.1	0.0
Other red oaks	54,606.8	1,515.6	2,683.6	3,355.3	4,818.2	5,475.2	6,300.3	6,121.5	4,800.6	4,932.6	4,271.6	5,150.2	2,462.4	1,599.4	1,120.4	0.0
Hickory	25,700.7	1,394.9	2,482.9	2,573.6	3,089.6	3,088.6	3,134.1	3,001.6	1,954.4	2,134.2	499.9	1,566.6	436.9	343.3	0.0	0.0
Hard maple	437.3	39.0	52.2	84.1	36.8	106.5	97.5	21.3	0.0	0.0	0.0	0.0	0.0	0.0	0.0	0.0
Soft maple	4,665.5	455.5	542.8	401.0	298.1	248.8	86.7	227.7	138.7	512.9	95.8	698.0	302.7	656.6	0.0	0.0
Beech	35.7	14.4	21.3	0.0	0.0	0.0	0.0	0.0	0.0	0.0	0.0	0.0	0.0	0.0	0.0	0.0
Sweetgum	5,066.7	251.9	504.5	715.1	614.6	655.8	598.0	616.9	280.6	392.4	347.7	89.2	0.0	0.0	0.0	0.0
Tupelo and blackgum	2,166.5	212.8	301.4	151.4	279.0	217.1	266.5	248.3	140.6	149.8	199.6	0.0	0.0	0.0	0.0	0.0
Ash	7,724.3	311.3	667.1	798.6	1,097.6	1,105.1	963.8	816.9	482.8	297.7	369.1	487.6	99.9	227.0	0.0	0.0
Cottonwood and aspen	1,197.7	0.0	0.0	21.2	50.4	105.0	236.6	106.3	135.0	427.9	115.4	0.0	0.0	0.0	0.0	0.0
Basswood	64.3	16.8	15.9	4.6	6.2	0.0	20.8	0.0	0.0	0.0	0.0	0.0	0.0	0.0	0.0	0.0
Black walnut	1,344.6	10.4	56.0	98.8	179.7	158.6	227.1	253.3	226.9	0.0	0.0	133.6	0.0	0.0	0.0	0.0
Other eastern soft hardwoods	23,985.1	2,081.6	3,554.7	2,717.1	2,829.2	2,537.2	2,333.2	1,538.7	1,527.2	996.7	1,207.2	890.6	312.1	950.0	509.6	0.0
Other eastern hard hardwoods	4,716.2	943.7	1,099.0	611.2	604.6	477.0	286.3	298.3	0.0	85.0	0.0	134.4	176.6	0.0	0.0	0.0
Eastern noncommercial hardwoods	4,419.8	907.6	1,026.9	655.2	527.0	365.2	329.0	127.8	93.5	58.1	43.0	121.1	165.4	0.0	0.0	0.0
Total hardwoods	220,250.4	9,800.6	16,761.3	19,707.3	25,566.8	26,495.9	25,863.9	23,810.8	18,999.0	15,922.3	9,722.7	14,004.2	5,291.8	4,677.4	2,880.1	746.5
All species	298,647.9	11,297.3	20,420.0	26,331.4	35,592.5	39,022.9	41,687.7	37,413.2	26,856.4	20,015.0	11,334.6	14,759.3	5,291.8	4,999.1	2,880.1	746.5

Numbers in rows and columns may not sum to totals due to rounding.

0.0 = no sample for the cell or a value of >0.0 but <0.05.

[a] Palm species have been included (species codes 906 to 915).

Table A.22.4—Merchantable dry weight of live trees on forest land by species group and diameter class, east Oklahoma, 2008

Species group[a]	All classes	Diameter class (inches at breast height)												
		5.0–6.9	7.0–8.9	9.0–10.9	11.0–12.9	13.0–14.9	15.0–16.9	17.0–18.9	19.0–20.9	21.0–24.9	25.0–28.9	29.0–32.9	33.0–36.9	37.0+
		thousand tons												
Softwood														
Loblolly and shortleaf pines	30,945.0	1,987.1	3,785.6	5,233.0	6,889.4	6,167.7	3,626.3	1,905.5	754.5	466.2	0.0	129.6	0.0	0.0
Cypress	0.0	0.0	0.0	0.0	0.0	0.0	0.0	0.0	0.0	0.0	0.0	0.0	0.0	0.0
Other eastern softwoods	1,876.0	565.8	494.0	404.6	182.2	131.0	60.3	38.1	0.0	0.0	0.0	0.0	0.0	0.0
Total softwoods	32,821.0	2,552.9	4,279.7	5,637.6	7,071.7	6,298.6	3,686.6	1,943.7	754.5	466.2	0.0	129.6	0.0	0.0
Hardwood														
Select white oaks	7,077.0	491.8	827.3	1,228.3	999.8	1,003.7	883.6	641.6	241.3	595.3	89.0	75.4	0.0	0.0
Select red oaks	3,847.7	203.8	373.2	501.4	403.3	504.9	431.2	357.0	89.5	302.8	56.6	149.4	168.5	306.1
Other white oaks	23,272.3	2,538.3	3,904.2	3,694.6	3,418.9	3,174.1	2,655.3	1,588.5	658.1	931.9	373.8	98.7	235.8	0.0
Other red oaks	19,968.0	1,314.3	1,973.7	2,319.8	2,637.7	2,471.9	1,868.3	1,867.0	1,516.5	2,045.6	938.1	574.9	440.2	0.0
Hickory	9,082.9	962.6	1,314.7	1,348.4	1,338.4	1,303.2	839.8	842.8	182.9	623.4	182.8	143.8	0.0	0.0
Hard maple	131.4	25.5	16.0	40.1	41.2	8.6	0.0	0.0	0.0	0.0	0.0	0.0	0.0	0.0
Soft maple	1,443.2	142.6	114.3	104.6	45.1	89.9	56.5	211.0	40.3	252.2	115.2	271.4	0.0	0.0
Sweetgum	1,736.9	243.1	244.2	271.8	263.1	263.6	114.5	164.1	133.1	39.5	0.0	0.0	0.0	0.0
Tupelo and blackgum	710.3	59.3	124.5	93.9	121.6	103.7	57.8	63.8	85.8	0.0	0.0	0.0	0.0	0.0
Ash	2,876.8	288.7	457.6	474.0	431.1	360.6	216.1	128.8	175.6	206.5	37.5	100.3	0.0	0.0
Cottonwood and aspen	511.5	7.5	20.1	43.7	101.0	45.7	58.2	185.2	50.1	0.0	0.0	0.0	0.0	0.0
Basswood	11.1	1.5	2.5	0.0	7.1	0.0	0.0	0.0	0.0	0.0	0.0	0.0	0.0	0.0
Black walnut	483.0	34.8	64.9	66.6	86.9	100.3	75.0	0.0	0.0	54.5	0.0	0.0	0.0	0.0
Other eastern soft hardwoods	7,405.1	1,005.9	1,173.4	1,061.5	959.9	624.2	622.7	412.7	474.0	350.9	134.2	363.7	222.1	0.0
Other eastern hard hardwoods	967.2	204.7	229.7	180.2	113.3	112.1	0.0	27.6	0.0	27.4	72.2	0.0	0.0	0.0
Eastern noncommercial hardwoods	899.5	219.1	200.5	141.9	125.4	57.4	35.0	16.4	14.9	41.7	47.3	0.0	0.0	0.0
Western woodland hardwoods	20.9	0.0	1.9	8.0	11.0	0.0	0.0	0.0	0.0	0.0	0.0	0.0	0.0	0.0
Total hardwoods	80,444.8	7,743.3	11,042.7	11,578.7	11,104.9	10,223.9	7,914.2	6,506.4	3,662.1	5,471.7	2,046.5	1,777.8	1,066.6	306.1
All species	113,265.8	10,296.2	15,322.4	17,216.3	18,176.5	16,522.5	11,600.7	8,450.0	4,416.6	5,937.9	2,046.5	1,907.4	1,066.6	306.1

Numbers in rows and columns may not sum to totals due to rounding.
0.0 = no sample for the cell or a value of > 0.0 but < 0.05.
[a] Palm species have been included (species codes 906 to 915).

Table A.22.5—Merchantable dry weight of live trees on timberland by species group and diameter class, east Oklahoma, 2008

Species group[a]		Diameter class (inches at breast height)												
	All classes	5.0–6.9	7.0–8.9	9.0–10.9	11.0–12.9	13.0–14.9	15.0–16.9	17.0–18.9	19.0–20.9	21.0–24.9	25.0–28.9	29.0–32.9	33.0–36.9	37.0+
						thousand tons								
Softwood														
Loblolly and shortleaf pines	29,688.1	1,959.0	3,719.8	5,054.2	6,758.7	5,890.5	3,383.9	1,748.3	711.4	332.7	0.0	129.6	0.0	0.0
Cypress	0.0	0.0	0.0	0.0	0.0	0.0	0.0	0.0	0.0	0.0	0.0	0.0	0.0	0.0
Other eastern softwoods	1,543.1	460.7	414.4	326.8	149.3	93.5	60.3	38.1	0.0	0.0	0.0	0.0	0.0	0.0
Total softwoods	31,231.2	2,419.7	4,134.2	5,380.9	6,907.9	5,984.0	3,444.2	1,786.4	711.4	332.7	0.0	129.6	0.0	0.0
Hardwood														
Select white oaks	6,613.6	458.1	777.2	1,139.5	903.2	933.1	837.0	621.7	241.3	538.0	89.0	75.4	0.0	0.0
Select red oaks	3,615.6	196.0	357.6	428.2	375.3	438.2	408.6	338.7	89.5	302.8	56.6	149.4	168.5	306.1
Other white oaks	19,228.3	1,853.0	3,017.4	3,025.9	2,936.9	2,615.3	2,288.6	1,316.3	595.2	915.4	329.7	98.7	235.8	0.0
Other red oaks	18,959.7	1,130.1	1,784.9	2,101.4	2,461.0	2,347.2	1,836.4	1,867.0	1,516.5	1,962.0	938.1	574.9	440.2	0.0
Hickory	8,376.5	814.2	1,146.9	1,201.8	1,240.9	1,202.0	795.0	842.8	182.9	623.4	182.8	143.8	0.0	0.0
Hard maple	121.6	25.5	13.6	40.1	33.8	8.6	0.0	0.0	0.0	0.0	0.0	0.0	0.0	0.0
Soft maple	1,417.7	137.5	110.6	97.6	35.4	89.9	56.5	211.0	40.3	252.2	115.2	271.4	0.0	0.0
Sweetgum	1,725.8	243.1	244.2	271.8	252.1	263.6	114.5	164.1	133.1	39.5	0.0	0.0	0.0	0.0
Tupelo and blackgum	672.0	53.1	110.3	87.0	110.5	103.7	57.8	63.8	85.8	0.0	0.0	0.0	0.0	0.0
Ash	2,751.8	276.6	443.5	459.1	401.0	345.2	204.4	128.8	149.0	206.5	37.5	100.3	0.0	0.0
Cottonwood and aspen	511.5	7.5	20.1	43.7	101.0	45.7	58.2	185.2	50.1	0.0	0.0	0.0	0.0	0.0
Basswood	11.1	1.5	2.5	0.0	7.1	0.0	0.0	0.0	0.0	0.0	0.0	0.0	0.0	0.0
Black walnut	475.7	33.4	64.9	60.7	86.9	100.3	75.0	0.0	0.0	54.5	0.0	0.0	0.0	0.0
Other eastern soft hardwoods	7,199.3	934.8	1,108.6	1,017.5	934.1	624.2	622.7	412.7	474.0	350.9	134.2	363.7	222.1	0.0
Other eastern hard hardwoods	951.5	196.6	222.0	180.2	113.3	112.1	0.0	27.6	0.0	27.4	72.2	0.0	0.0	0.0
Eastern noncommercial hardwoods	877.5	212.0	196.8	137.6	125.4	50.5	35.0	16.4	14.9	41.7	47.3	0.0	0.0	0.0
Total hardwoods	73,509.1	6,573.1	9,621.2	10,292.1	10,117.7	9,279.5	7,389.6	6,196.0	3,572.5	5,314.4	2,002.5	1,777.8	1,066.6	306.1
All species	104,740.3	8,992.9	13,755.5	15,673.0	17,025.7	15,263.5	10,833.8	7,982.4	4,283.9	5,647.1	2,002.5	1,907.4	1,066.6	306.1

Numbers in rows and columns may not sum to totals due to rounding.

0.0 = no sample for the cell or a value of > 0.0 but < 0.05.

[a] Palm species have been included (species codes 906 to 915).

Table A.23—Total carbon[a] of live trees on forest land by ownership class and land status, east Oklahoma, 2008

Ownership class	All forest land	Unreserved			Reserved		
		Total	Timber-land	Unpro-ductive	Total	Pro-ductive	Unpro-ductive
		thousand tons					
U.S. Forest Service							
National forest	6,825.4	6,180.9	6,101.2	79.8	644.5	644.5	0.0
Total	6,825.4	6,180.9	6,101.2	79.8	644.5	644.5	0.0
Other Federal							
U.S. Fish and Wildlife Service	276.0	276.0	276.0	0.0	0.0	0.0	0.0
Dept. of Defense/Dept. of Energy	4,318.8	4,318.8	4,096.3	222.5	0.0	0.0	0.0
Other Federal	997.3	997.3	997.3	0.0	0.0	0.0	0.0
Total	5,592.1	5,592.1	5,369.7	222.5	0.0	0.0	0.0
State and local government							
State	3,173.3	2,493.9	2,382.4	111.5	679.4	679.4	0.0
Local	485.3	485.3	414.9	70.4	0.0	0.0	0.0
Total	3,658.6	2,979.2	2,797.3	181.9	679.4	679.4	0.0
Forest industry							
Corporate	7,608.8	7,608.8	7,608.8	0.0	0.0	0.0	0.0
Total	7,608.8	7,608.8	7,608.8	0.0	0.0	0.0	0.0
Nonindustrial private							
Corporate	11,043.3	11,043.3	10,451.4	591.9	0.0	0.0	0.0
Conservation/natural resources organization	196.1	196.1	196.1	0.0	0.0	0.0	0.0
Unincorporated partnership/ association/club	2,113.6	2,113.6	1,858.9	254.7	0.0	0.0	0.0
Native American	888.4	888.4	888.4	0.0	0.0	0.0	0.0
Individual	43,338.7	43,338.7	39,390.2	3,948.5	0.0	0.0	0.0
Total	57,580.1	57,580.1	52,785.0	4,795.1	0.0	0.0	0.0
All classes	81,265.1	79,941.2	74,662.0	5,279.3	1,323.8	1,323.8	0.0

Numbers in rows and columns may not sum to totals due to rounding.

0.0 = no sample for the cell or a value of > 0.0 but < 0.05.

[a] Estimates of carbon calculated by multiplying aboveground dry tree biomass by 0.5.

Table A.24—Average annual net growth of live trees by ownership class and land status, east Oklahoma, 2008 (1993–2008)

Ownership class	Timber-land	Forest land
	million cubic feet	
U.S. Forest Service		
National forest	12.5	0.0
Total	12.5	0.0
Other Federal		
U.S. Fish and Wildlife Service	0.4	0.0
Dept. of Defense/Dept. of Energy	6.3	0.0
Other Federal	0.3	0.0
Total	7.0	0.0
State and local government		
State	4.0	0.0
Local	1.4	0.0
Total	5.4	0.0
Forest industry		
Corporate	37.3	0.0
Total	37.3	0.0
Nonindustrial private		
Corporate	27.8	0.0
Conservation/natural resources organization	-0.2	0.0
Unincorporated partnership/ association/club	5.7	0.0
Native American	0.8	0.0
Individual	79.6	0.0
Total	113.7	0.0
All classes	175.8	0.0

Note: The reserved forest land was not sampled in the 1992 survey; therefore, growth, removals, and mortality estimates are not available for forest land for this survey.

Numbers in rows and columns may not sum to totals due to rounding.

0.0 = no sample for the cell or a value of > 0.0 but < 0.05.

Table A.25—Average annual net growth of live trees on forest land by forest-type group and stand-size class, east Oklahoma, 2008 (1993–2008)

Forest-type group	All size classes	Stand-size class			
		Large diameter	Medium diameter	Small diameter	Non-stocked
		million cubic feet			
Softwood types					
Loblolly-shortleaf pine	0.0	0.0	0.0	0.0	0.0
Other eastern softwoods	0.0	0.0	0.0	0.0	0.0
Total softwoods	0.0	0.0	0.0	0.0	0.0
Hardwood types					
Oak-pine	0.0	0.0	0.0	0.0	0.0
Oak-hickory	0.0	0.0	0.0	0.0	0.0
Oak-gum-cypress	0.0	0.0	0.0	0.0	0.0
Elm-ash-cottonwood	0.0	0.0	0.0	0.0	0.0
Total hardwoods	0.0	0.0	0.0	0.0	0.0
All groups	0.0	0.0	0.0	0.0	0.0

Note: The reserved forest land was not sampled in the 1992 survey; therefore, growth, removals, and mortality estimates are not available for forest land for this survey.

Numbers in rows and columns may not sum to totals due to rounding.

0.0 = no sample for the cell or a value of > 0.0 but < 0.05.

Table A.25.1—Average annual net growth of live trees on timberland by forest-type group and stand-size class, east Oklahoma, 2008 (1993–2008)

Forest-type group	All size classes	Stand-size class			
		Large diameter	Medium diameter	Small diameter	Non-stocked
		million cubic feet			
Softwood types					
Loblolly-shortleaf pine	65.1	14.5	39.5	11.2	0.0
Other eastern softwoods	1.9	0.9	0.5	0.5	0.0
Total softwoods	67.1	15.4	40.1	11.6	0.0
Hardwood types					
Oak-pine	27.5	4.9	11.1	11.5	0.0
Oak-hickory	70.2	18.9	27.4	23.9	0.0
Oak-gum-cypress	6.6	0.7	3.9	1.9	0.0
Elm-ash-cottonwood	4.6	-0.3	3.3	1.6	0.0
Total hardwoods	108.8	24.2	45.7	38.9	0.0
All groups	175.8	39.5	85.7	50.5	0.0

Numbers in rows and columns may not sum to totals due to rounding.

0.0 = no sample for the cell or a value of > 0.0 but < 0.05.

Table A.26—Average annual net growth of live trees on forest land by species group and ownership group, east Oklahoma, 2008 (1993–2008)

Species group[a]	All ownerships	U.S. Forest Service	Other Federal	State and local government	Forest industry	Nonindustrial private
				million cubic feet		
Softwood						
Loblolly and shortleaf pines	0.0	0.0	0.0	0.0	0.0	0.0
Cypress	0.0	0.0	0.0	0.0	0.0	0.0
Other eastern softwoods	0.0	0.0	0.0	0.0	0.0	0.0
Total softwoods	0.0	0.0	0.0	0.0	0.0	0.0
Hardwood						
Select white oaks	0.0	0.0	0.0	0.0	0.0	0.0
Select red oaks	0.0	0.0	0.0	0.0	0.0	0.0
Other white oaks	0.0	0.0	0.0	0.0	0.0	0.0
Other red oaks	0.0	0.0	0.0	0.0	0.0	0.0
Hickory	0.0	0.0	0.0	0.0	0.0	0.0
Hard maple	0.0	0.0	0.0	0.0	0.0	0.0
Soft maple	0.0	0.0	0.0	0.0	0.0	0.0
Sweetgum	0.0	0.0	0.0	0.0	0.0	0.0
Tupelo and blackgum	0.0	0.0	0.0	0.0	0.0	0.0
Ash	0.0	0.0	0.0	0.0	0.0	0.0
Cottonwood and aspen	0.0	0.0	0.0	0.0	0.0	0.0
Basswood	0.0	0.0	0.0	0.0	0.0	0.0
Black walnut	0.0	0.0	0.0	0.0	0.0	0.0
Other eastern soft hardwoods	0.0	0.0	0.0	0.0	0.0	0.0
Other eastern hard hardwoods	0.0	0.0	0.0	0.0	0.0	0.0
Eastern noncommercial hardwoods	0.0	0.0	0.0	0.0	0.0	0.0
Other western hardwoods	0.0	0.0	0.0	0.0	0.0	0.0
Total hardwoods	0.0	0.0	0.0	0.0	0.0	0.0
All species	0.0	0.0	0.0	0.0	0.0	0.0

Note: The reserved forest land was not sampled in the 1992 survey; therefore, growth, removals, and mortality estimates are not available for forest land for this survey.

Numbers in rows and columns may not sum to totals due to rounding.

0.0 = no sample for the cell or a value of > 0.0 but < 0.05.

[a] Palm species have been included (species codes 906 to 915).

Table A.26.1—Average annual net growth of live trees on timberland by species group and ownership group, east Oklahoma, 2008 (1993–2008)

Species group[a]	All ownerships	U.S. Forest Service	Other Federal	State and local government	Forest industry	Nonindustrial private
				million cubic feet		
Softwood						
Loblolly and shortleaf pines	87.6	10.0	0.5	2.3	31.6	43.1
Cypress	0.1	0.0	0.0	0.0	0.0	0.0
Other eastern softwoods	5.8	0.2	0.4	0.2	0.0	4.9
Total softwoods	93.5	10.2	1.0	2.5	31.6	48.1
Hardwood						
Select white oaks	6.4	0.5	0.5	0.1	1.2	4.1
Select red oaks	4.9	0.1	1.0	0.3	0.5	2.9
Other white oaks	22.9	1.0	1.0	0.6	0.5	19.8
Other red oaks	14.1	-0.3	1.9	0.2	1.1	11.2
Hickory	10.6	0.2	1.3	0.3	0.8	8.0
Hard maple	0.1	0.0	0.0	0.0	0.1	0.0
Soft maple	2.4	0.3	0.1	0.4	0.4	1.2
Sweetgum	5.1	0.4	0.9	0.0	0.8	3.0
Tupelo and blackgum	1.0	0.0	0.0	0.1	0.2	0.8
Ash	4.3	0.0	0.4	0.2	0.0	3.7
Cottonwood and aspen	-1.4	0.0	-1.7	0.0	0.0	0.3
Basswood	0.0	0.0	0.0	0.0	-0.1	0.0
Black walnut	1.2	0.0	-0.1	0.2	0.0	1.1
Other eastern soft hardwoods	8.3	-0.1	0.8	0.1	0.3	7.2
Other eastern hard hardwoods	0.8	-0.1	-0.1	0.3	0.0	0.7
Eastern noncommercial hardwoods	1.6	0.0	0.0	0.1	-0.1	1.6
Other western hardwoods	0.0	0.0	0.0	0.0	0.0	0.0
Total hardwoods	82.4	2.2	6.0	2.9	5.7	65.6
All species	175.8	12.5	7.0	5.4	37.3	113.7

Numbers in rows and columns may not sum to totals due to rounding.

0.0 = no sample for the cell or a value of >0.0 but <0.05.

[a] Palm species have been included (species codes 906 to 915).

Table A.27—Average annual net growth of growing-stock trees on timberland by species group and ownership group, east Oklahoma, 2008 (1993–2008)

Species group[a]	All ownerships	U.S. Forest Service	Other Federal	State and local government	Forest industry	Nonindustrial private
				million cubic feet		
Softwood						
Loblolly and shortleaf pines	83.6	9.7	0.5	2.3	30.7	40.3
Cypress	0.0	0.0	0.0	0.0	0.0	0.0
Other eastern softwoods	3.6	0.2	0.4	0.0	0.0	2.9
Total softwoods	87.2	10.0	1.0	2.3	30.7	43.2
Hardwood						
Select white oaks	4.1	0.3	0.2	0.0	0.9	2.8
Select red oaks	3.7	0.1	1.0	0.5	0.2	1.9
Other white oaks	15.6	0.8	0.9	0.5	0.4	13.1
Other red oaks	13.2	-0.2	1.6	0.3	0.6	10.9
Hickory	6.9	0.2	0.9	0.2	0.7	4.9
Hard maple	0.0	0.0	0.0	0.0	0.0	0.0
Soft maple	1.5	0.0	0.0	0.4	0.2	1.0
Sweetgum	3.2	0.2	0.8	0.0	0.7	1.5
Tupelo and blackgum	0.6	0.0	0.0	0.0	0.2	0.4
Ash	0.9	0.0	0.0	0.0	0.0	0.9
Cottonwood and aspen	-1.6	0.0	-1.7	0.0	0.0	0.1
Basswood	-0.1	0.0	0.0	0.0	-0.1	0.0
Black walnut	0.9	0.0	0.0	0.2	0.0	0.7
Other eastern soft hardwoods	2.9	-0.1	-0.1	0.0	0.1	3.0
Other eastern hard hardwoods	0.5	0.0	0.0	0.2	0.0	0.3
Eastern noncommercial hardwoods	0.0	0.0	0.0	0.0	0.0	0.0
Other western hardwoods	0.0	0.0	0.0	0.0	0.0	0.0
Total hardwoods	52.4	1.2	3.5	2.5	4.0	41.3
All species	139.6	11.2	4.5	4.7	34.7	84.5

Numbers in rows and columns may not sum to totals due to rounding.

0.0 = no sample for the cell or a value of >0.0 but <0.05.

[a] Palm species have been included (species codes 906 to 915).

Table A.27.1—Average annual net growth of sawtimber on timberland by species group and ownership group, east Oklahoma, 2008 (1993–2008)

Species group[a]	All ownerships	U.S. Forest Service	Other Federal	State and local government	Forest industry	Nonindustrial private
				million board feet[b]		
Softwood						
Loblolly and shortleaf pines	378.1	41.7	5.3	14.1	133.2	183.7
Cypress	0.3	0.0	0.1	0.0	0.0	0.2
Other eastern softwoods	3.8	0.0	0.7	0.0	0.0	3.2
Total softwoods	382.2	41.7	6.1	14.1	133.2	187.1
Hardwood						
Select white oaks	14.0	1.0	0.6	0.2	3.0	9.2
Select red oaks	15.5	0.4	2.9	3.1	1.5	7.6
Other white oaks	39.4	1.3	2.5	1.7	0.6	33.2
Other red oaks	57.4	-0.6	6.3	2.1	-1.0	50.7
Hickory	20.4	1.7	3.4	0.2	0.0	15.2
Hard maple	0.0	0.0	0.0	0.0	0.0	0.0
Soft maple	5.7	0.0	0.0	2.7	0.0	3.0
Sweetgum	5.3	0.4	1.0	0.0	0.2	3.7
Tupelo and blackgum	1.8	0.0	0.0	0.2	0.3	1.2
Ash	7.2	0.0	0.7	0.1	0.4	5.9
Cottonwood and aspen	-9.0	0.0	-10.0	0.0	0.0	1.0
Basswood	-0.2	0.0	0.0	0.0	-0.2	0.0
Black walnut	2.4	0.0	0.0	0.8	0.0	1.6
Other eastern soft hardwoods	7.7	-0.3	0.8	0.7	0.5	6.0
Other eastern hard hardwoods	1.3	0.0	0.0	0.0	0.0	1.3
Eastern noncommercial hardwoods	0.0	0.0	0.0	0.0	0.0	0.0
Other western hardwoods	0.0	0.0	0.0	0.0	0.0	0.0
Total hardwoods	168.8	4.0	8.1	11.8	5.3	139.6
All species	551.0	45.7	14.2	25.9	138.5	326.7

Numbers in rows and columns may not sum to totals due to rounding.

0.0 = no sample for the cell or a value of > 0.0 but < 0.05.

[a] Palm species have been included (species codes 906 to 915).

[b] International ¼-inch rule.

Table A.28—Average annual mortality of live trees by ownership class and land status, east Oklahoma, 2008 (1993–2008)

Ownership class	Timber-land	Forest land
	million cubic feet	
U.S. Forest Service		
National forest	3.8	0.0
Total	3.8	0.0
Other Federal		
U.S. Fish and Wildlife Service	0.1	0.0
Dept. of Defense/Dept. of Energy	6.2	0.0
Other Federal	2.0	0.0
Total	8.3	0.0
State and local government		
State	2.6	0.0
Local	0.1	0.0
Total	2.7	0.0
Forest industry		
Corporate	3.8	0.0
Total	3.8	0.0
Nonindustrial private		
Corporate	9.2	0.0
Conservation/natural resources organization	0.8	0.0
Unincorporated partnership/ association/club	2.4	0.0
Native American	0.8	0.0
Individual	41.6	0.0
Total	54.7	0.0
All classes	73.4	0.0

Note: The reserved forest land was not sampled in the 1992 survey; therefore, growth, removals, and mortality estimates are not available for forest land for this survey.

Numbers in rows and columns may not sum to totals due to rounding.

0.0 = no sample for the cell or a value of > 0.0 but < 0.05.

Table A.29—Average annual mortality of live trees on forest land by forest-type group and stand-size class, east Oklahoma, 2008 (1993–2008)

Forest-type group	Stand-size class				
	All size classes	Large diameter	Medium diameter	Small diameter	Non-stocked
	million cubic feet				
Softwood types					
Loblolly-shortleaf pine	0.0	0.0	0.0	0.0	0.0
Other eastern softwoods	0.0	0.0	0.0	0.0	0.0
Total softwoods	0.0	0.0	0.0	0.0	0.0
Hardwood types					
Oak-pine	0.0	0.0	0.0	0.0	0.0
Oak-hickory	0.0	0.0	0.0	0.0	0.0
Oak-gum-cypress	0.0	0.0	0.0	0.0	0.0
Elm-ash-cottonwood	0.0	0.0	0.0	0.0	0.0
Total hardwoods	0.0	0.0	0.0	0.0	0.0
All groups	0.0	0.0	0.0	0.0	0.0

Note: The reserved forest land was not sampled in the 1992 survey; therefore, growth, removals, and mortality estimates are not available for forest land for this survey.
Numbers in rows and columns may not sum to totals due to rounding.
0.0 = no sample for the cell or a value of > 0.0 but < 0.05.

Table A.29.1—Average annual mortality of live trees on timberland by forest-type group and stand-size class, east Oklahoma, 2008 (1993–2008)

Forest-type group	Stand-size class				
	All size classes	Large diameter	Medium diameter	Small diameter	Non-stocked
	million cubic feet				
Softwood types					
Loblolly-shortleaf pine	11.6	6.4	4.2	1.0	0.0
Other eastern softwoods	0.4	0.4	0.0	0.0	0.0
Total softwoods	12.0	6.8	4.2	1.0	0.0
Hardwood types					
Oak-pine	7.9	2.8	4.2	0.9	0.0
Oak-hickory	39.0	11.9	21.2	6.0	0.0
Oak-gum-cypress	7.8	5.9	1.4	0.6	0.0
Elm-ash-cottonwood	6.6	4.1	2.2	0.3	0.0
Total hardwoods	61.4	24.6	29.0	7.8	0.0
All groups	73.4	31.4	33.2	8.8	0.0

Numbers in rows and columns may not sum to totals due to rounding.
0.0 = no sample for the cell or a value of > 0.0 but < 0.05.

Table A.30—Average annual mortality of live trees on forest land by species group and ownership group, east Oklahoma, 2008 (1993–2008)

Species group[a]	All ownerships	U.S. Forest Service	Other Federal	State and local government	Forest industry	Nonindustrial private
				million cubic feet		
Softwood						
Loblolly and shortleaf pines	0.0	0.0	0.0	0.0	0.0	0.0
Cypress	0.0	0.0	0.0	0.0	0.0	0.0
Other eastern softwoods	0.0	0.0	0.0	0.0	0.0	0.0
Total softwoods	0.0	0.0	0.0	0.0	0.0	0.0
Hardwood						
Select white oaks	0.0	0.0	0.0	0.0	0.0	0.0
Select red oaks	0.0	0.0	0.0	0.0	0.0	0.0
Other white oaks	0.0	0.0	0.0	0.0	0.0	0.0
Other red oaks	0.0	0.0	0.0	0.0	0.0	0.0
Hickory	0.0	0.0	0.0	0.0	0.0	0.0
Hard maple	0.0	0.0	0.0	0.0	0.0	0.0
Soft maple	0.0	0.0	0.0	0.0	0.0	0.0
Sweetgum	0.0	0.0	0.0	0.0	0.0	0.0
Tupelo and blackgum	0.0	0.0	0.0	0.0	0.0	0.0
Ash	0.0	0.0	0.0	0.0	0.0	0.0
Cottonwood and aspen	0.0	0.0	0.0	0.0	0.0	0.0
Basswood	0.0	0.0	0.0	0.0	0.0	0.0
Black walnut	0.0	0.0	0.0	0.0	0.0	0.0
Other eastern soft hardwoods	0.0	0.0	0.0	0.0	0.0	0.0
Other eastern hard hardwoods	0.0	0.0	0.0	0.0	0.0	0.0
Eastern noncommercial hardwoods	0.0	0.0	0.0	0.0	0.0	0.0
Other western hardwoods	0.0	0.0	0.0	0.0	0.0	0.0
Total hardwoods	0.0	0.0	0.0	0.0	0.0	0.0
All species	0.0	0.0	0.0	0.0	0.0	0.0

Note: The reserved forest land was not sampled in the 1992 survey; therefore, growth, removals, and mortality estimates are not available for forest land for this survey.

Numbers in rows and columns may not sum to totals due to rounding.

0.0 = no sample for the cell or a value of > 0.0 but < 0.05.

[a] Palm species have been included (species codes 906 to 915).

Table A.30.1—Average annual mortality of live trees on timberland by species group and ownership group, east Oklahoma, 2008 (1993–2008)

Species group[a]	All ownerships	U.S. Forest Service	Other Federal	State and local government	Forest industry	Nonindustrial private
				million cubic feet		
Softwood						
Loblolly and shortleaf pines	12.9	1.6	1.6	0.2	1.7	7.9
Cypress	0.0	0.0	0.0	0.0	0.0	0.0
Other eastern softwoods	0.3	0.0	0.0	0.0	0.0	0.3
Total softwoods	13.2	1.6	1.6	0.2	1.7	8.2
Hardwood						
Select white oaks	2.3	0.4	0.0	0.1	0.2	1.7
Select red oaks	3.1	0.1	0.1	0.3	0.2	2.4
Other white oaks	9.7	0.1	1.2	0.6	0.1	7.8
Other red oaks	21.7	1.1	1.2	0.6	0.8	18.1
Hickory	4.2	0.3	0.2	0.2	0.3	3.2
Hard maple	0.1	0.0	0.0	0.0	0.0	0.1
Soft maple	0.7	0.0	0.1	0.0	0.0	0.6
Sweetgum	0.8	0.0	0.1	0.0	0.1	0.6
Tupelo and blackgum	0.2	0.0	0.0	0.0	0.0	0.2
Ash	2.8	0.0	0.5	0.2	0.2	2.0
Cottonwood and aspen	2.8	0.0	2.1	0.0	0.0	0.7
Basswood	0.1	0.0	0.0	0.0	0.1	0.1
Black walnut	0.2	0.0	0.1	0.0	0.0	0.1
Other eastern soft hardwoods	8.8	0.2	0.9	0.4	0.1	7.2
Other eastern hard hardwoods	2.0	0.1	0.3	0.1	0.0	1.5
Eastern noncommercial hardwoods	0.6	0.0	0.0	0.0	0.1	0.5
Other western hardwoods	0.0	0.0	0.0	0.0	0.0	0.0
Total hardwoods	60.2	2.3	6.7	2.5	2.2	46.5
All species	73.4	3.8	8.3	2.7	3.8	54.7

Numbers in rows and columns may not sum to totals due to rounding.

0.0 = no sample for the cell or a value of > 0.0 but < 0.05.

[a] Palm species have been included (species codes 906 to 915).

Table A.31—Average annual mortality of growing-stock trees on timberland by species group and ownership group, east Oklahoma, 2008 (1993–2008)

Species group[a]	All ownerships	U.S. Forest Service	Other Federal	State and local government	Forest industry	Nonindustrial private
				million cubic feet		
Softwood						
Loblolly and shortleaf pines	11.8	1.4	1.5	0.2	1.6	7.1
Cypress	0.0	0.0	0.0	0.0	0.0	0.0
Other eastern softwoods	0.2	0.0	0.0	0.0	0.0	0.2
Total softwoods	12.0	1.4	1.5	0.2	1.6	7.3
Hardwood						
Select white oaks	1.3	0.2	0.0	0.0	0.2	0.9
Select red oaks	2.0	0.1	0.1	0.2	0.2	1.4
Other white oaks	4.3	0.0	0.7	0.2	0.0	3.4
Other red oaks	9.0	0.7	0.2	0.1	0.7	7.3
Hickory	1.9	0.2	0.1	0.1	0.2	1.3
Hard maple	0.0	0.0	0.0	0.0	0.0	0.0
Soft maple	0.4	0.0	0.0	0.0	0.0	0.4
Sweetgum	0.6	0.0	0.1	0.0	0.1	0.3
Tupelo and blackgum	0.1	0.0	0.0	0.0	0.0	0.1
Ash	1.9	0.0	0.4	0.1	0.2	1.3
Cottonwood and aspen	2.5	0.0	2.1	0.0	0.0	0.4
Basswood	0.1	0.0	0.0	0.0	0.1	0.1
Black walnut	0.0	0.0	0.0	0.0	0.0	0.0
Other eastern soft hardwoods	4.6	0.1	0.5	0.2	0.0	3.7
Other eastern hard hardwoods	0.6	0.0	0.1	0.1	0.0	0.5
Eastern noncommercial hardwoods	0.0	0.0	0.0	0.0	0.0	0.0
Other western hardwoods	0.0	0.0	0.0	0.0	0.0	0.0
Total hardwoods	29.3	1.5	4.2	0.9	1.7	21.0
All species	41.3	2.9	5.7	1.1	3.3	28.3

Numbers in rows and columns may not sum to totals due to rounding.

0.0 = no sample for the cell or a value of >0.0 but <0.05.

[a] Palm species have been included (species codes 906 to 915).

Table A.31.1—Average annual mortality of sawtimber on timberland by species group and ownership group, east Oklahoma, 2008 (1993–2008)

Species group[a]	All ownerships	U.S. Forest Service	Other Federal	State and local government	Forest industry	Nonindustrial private
				million board feet[b]		
Softwood						
Loblolly and shortleaf pines	32.8	3.3	4.7	0.9	7.0	16.9
Cypress	0.0	0.0	0.0	0.0	0.0	0.0
Other eastern softwoods	0.3	0.0	0.0	0.0	0.0	0.3
Total softwoods	33.0	3.3	4.7	0.9	7.0	17.2
Hardwood						
Select white oaks	1.7	0.0	0.0	0.0	0.3	1.3
Select red oaks	6.7	0.4	0.6	0.5	0.8	4.5
Other white oaks	6.3	0.0	0.5	0.3	0.0	5.5
Other red oaks	23.3	2.7	0.5	0.0	2.7	17.4
Hickory	3.8	0.2	0.0	0.0	0.9	2.7
Hard maple	0.0	0.0	0.0	0.0	0.0	0.0
Soft maple	2.8	0.0	0.0	0.0	0.0	2.8
Sweetgum	1.3	0.0	0.3	0.0	0.0	1.0
Tupelo and blackgum	0.0	0.0	0.0	0.0	0.0	0.0
Ash	5.3	0.0	0.5	0.5	0.7	3.6
Cottonwood and aspen	12.7	0.0	12.3	0.0	0.0	0.4
Basswood	0.2	0.0	0.0	0.0	0.2	0.0
Black walnut	0.0	0.0	0.0	0.0	0.0	0.0
Other eastern soft hardwoods	12.9	0.4	1.7	0.4	0.0	10.5
Other eastern hard hardwoods	0.0	0.0	0.0	0.0	0.0	0.0
Eastern noncommercial hardwoods	0.0	0.0	0.0	0.0	0.0	0.0
Other western hardwoods	0.0	0.0	0.0	0.0	0.0	0.0
Total hardwoods	77.1	3.7	16.5	1.7	5.6	49.6
All species	110.1	7.0	21.2	2.5	12.6	66.8

Numbers in rows and columns may not sum to totals due to rounding.

0.0 = no sample for the cell or a value of > 0.0 but < 0.05.

[a] Palm species have been included (species codes 906 to 915).

[b] International ¼-inch rule.

Table A.32—Average annual removals of live trees by ownership class and land status, east Oklahoma, 2008 (1993–2008)

Ownership class	Timber-land	Forest land
	million cubic feet	
U.S. Forest Service		
National forest	3.2	0.0
Total	3.2	0.0
Other Federal		
U.S. Fish and Wildlife Service	0.7	0.0
Dept. of Defense/Dept. of Energy	1.3	0.0
Total	2.0	0.0
State and local government		
State	0.3	0.0
Local	0.9	0.0
Total	1.2	0.0
Forest industry		
Corporate	30.9	0.0
Total	30.9	0.0
Nonindustrial private		
Corporate	22.2	0.0
Unincorporated partnership/ association/club	3.5	0.0
Native American	0.1	0.0
Individual	65.6	0.0
Total	91.3	0.0
All classes	128.8	0.0

Note: The reserved forest land was not sampled in the 1992 survey; therefore, growth, removals, and mortality estimates are not available for forest land for this survey.

Numbers in rows and columns may not sum to totals due to rounding.

0.0 = no sample for the cell or a value of > 0.0 but < 0.05.

Table A.33—Average annual removals of live trees on forest land by forest-type group and stand-size class, east Oklahoma, 2008 (1993–2008)

		Stand-size class			
Forest-type group	All size classes	Large diameter	Medium diameter	Small diameter	Non-stocked
	million cubic feet				
Softwood types					
Loblolly-shortleaf pine	0.0	0.0	0.0	0.0	0.0
Other eastern softwoods	0.0	0.0	0.0	0.0	0.0
Total softwoods	0.0	0.0	0.0	0.0	0.0
Hardwood types					
Oak-pine	0.0	0.0	0.0	0.0	0.0
Oak-hickory	0.0	0.0	0.0	0.0	0.0
Oak-gum-cypress	0.0	0.0	0.0	0.0	0.0
Elm-ash-cottonwood	0.0	0.0	0.0	0.0	0.0
Total hardwoods	0.0	0.0	0.0	0.0	0.0
All groups	0.0	0.0	0.0	0.0	0.0

Note: The reserved forest land was not sampled in the 1992 survey; therefore, growth, removals, and mortality estimates are not available for forest land for this survey.

Numbers in rows and columns may not sum to totals due to rounding.

0.0 = no sample for the cell or a value of > 0.0 but < 0.05.

Table A.33.1—Average annual removals of live trees on timberland by forest-type group and stand-size class, east Oklahoma, 2008 (1993–2008)

		Stand-size class			
Forest-type group	All size classes	Large diameter	Medium diameter	Small diameter	Non-stocked
	million cubic feet				
Softwood types					
Loblolly-shortleaf pine	60.6	30.1	27.6	2.8	0.0
Other eastern softwoods	1.1	0.5	0.0	0.5	0.0
Total softwoods	61.7	30.7	27.6	3.4	0.0
Hardwood types					
Oak-pine	15.4	4.0	8.6	2.8	0.0
Oak-hickory	43.7	14.1	22.7	6.9	0.0
Oak-gum-cypress	5.2	3.5	0.8	0.9	0.0
Elm-ash-cottonwood	2.9	2.0	0.9	0.0	0.0
Total hardwoods	67.1	23.6	33.1	10.5	0.0
All groups	128.8	54.2	60.7	13.9	0.0

Numbers in rows and columns may not sum to totals due to rounding.

0.0 = no sample for the cell or a value of > 0.0 but < 0.05.

Table A.34—Average annual removals of live trees on forest land by species group and ownership group, east Oklahoma, 2008 (1993–2008)

Species group[a]	All ownerships	U.S. Forest Service	Other Federal	State and local government	Forest industry	Nonindustrial private
				million cubic feet		
Softwood						
Loblolly and shortleaf pines	0.0	0.0	0.0	0.0	0.0	0.0
Cypress	0.0	0.0	0.0	0.0	0.0	0.0
Other eastern softwoods	0.0	0.0	0.0	0.0	0.0	0.0
Total softwoods	0.0	0.0	0.0	0.0	0.0	0.0
Hardwood						
Select white oaks	0.0	0.0	0.0	0.0	0.0	0.0
Select red oaks	0.0	0.0	0.0	0.0	0.0	0.0
Other white oaks	0.0	0.0	0.0	0.0	0.0	0.0
Other red oaks	0.0	0.0	0.0	0.0	0.0	0.0
Hickory	0.0	0.0	0.0	0.0	0.0	0.0
Hard maple	0.0	0.0	0.0	0.0	0.0	0.0
Soft maple	0.0	0.0	0.0	0.0	0.0	0.0
Sweetgum	0.0	0.0	0.0	0.0	0.0	0.0
Tupelo and blackgum	0.0	0.0	0.0	0.0	0.0	0.0
Ash	0.0	0.0	0.0	0.0	0.0	0.0
Cottonwood and aspen	0.0	0.0	0.0	0.0	0.0	0.0
Basswood	0.0	0.0	0.0	0.0	0.0	0.0
Black walnut	0.0	0.0	0.0	0.0	0.0	0.0
Other eastern soft hardwoods	0.0	0.0	0.0	0.0	0.0	0.0
Other eastern hard hardwoods	0.0	0.0	0.0	0.0	0.0	0.0
Eastern noncommercial hardwoods	0.0	0.0	0.0	0.0	0.0	0.0
Other western hardwoods	0.0	0.0	0.0	0.0	0.0	0.0
Total hardwoods	0.0	0.0	0.0	0.0	0.0	0.0
All species	0.0	0.0	0.0	0.0	0.0	0.0

Note: The reserved forest land was not sampled in the 1992 survey; therefore, growth, removals, and mortality estimates are not available for forest land for this survey.

Numbers in rows and columns may not sum to totals due to rounding.

0.0 = no sample for the cell or a value of > 0.0 but < 0.05.

[a] Palm species have been included (species codes 906 to 915).

Table A.34.1—Average annual removals of live trees on timberland by species group and ownership group, east Oklahoma, 2008 (1993–2008)

Species group[a]	All ownerships	U.S. Forest Service	Other Federal	State and local government	Forest industry	Nonindustrial private
				million cubic feet		
Softwood						
Loblolly and shortleaf pines	69.4	2.2	0.0	0.3	25.2	41.6
Cypress	0.2	0.0	0.2	0.0	0.0	0.0
Other eastern softwoods	1.7	0.3	0.0	0.0	0.0	1.3
Total softwoods	71.2	2.5	0.2	0.3	25.2	42.9
Hardwood						
Select white oaks	4.3	0.2	0.0	0.0	0.7	3.4
Select red oaks	2.9	0.0	0.0	0.0	0.2	2.7
Other white oaks	14.4	0.2	1.2	0.5	1.2	11.3
Other red oaks	15.6	0.2	0.0	0.3	1.3	13.7
Hickory	7.5	0.0	0.4	0.2	1.1	5.9
Hard maple	0.1	0.0	0.0	0.0	0.0	0.1
Soft maple	0.3	0.0	0.0	0.0	0.1	0.2
Sweetgum	1.0	0.1	0.0	0.0	0.3	0.6
Tupelo and blackgum	0.4	0.0	0.0	0.0	0.2	0.1
Ash	2.8	0.0	0.1	0.0	0.2	2.6
Cottonwood and aspen	0.0	0.0	0.0	0.0	0.0	0.0
Basswood	0.0	0.0	0.0	0.0	0.0	0.0
Black walnut	0.3	0.0	0.0	0.0	0.0	0.3
Other eastern soft hardwoods	6.2	0.0	0.2	0.0	0.3	5.7
Other eastern hard hardwoods	0.8	0.0	0.0	0.0	0.1	0.8
Eastern noncommercial hardwoods	1.1	0.0	0.0	0.0	0.0	1.1
Other western hardwoods	0.0	0.0	0.0	0.0	0.0	0.0
Total hardwoods	57.6	0.7	1.8	0.9	5.7	48.4
All species	128.8	3.2	2.1	1.3	30.9	91.3

Numbers in rows and columns may not sum to totals due to rounding.

0.0 = no sample for the cell or a value of > 0.0 but < 0.05.

[a] Palm species have been included (species codes 906 to 915).

Table A.35—Average annual removals of growing-stock trees on timberland by species group and ownership group, east Oklahoma, 2008 (1993–2008)

Species group[a]	All ownerships	U.S. Forest Service	Other Federal	State and local government	Forest industry	Nonindustrial private
				million cubic feet		
Softwood						
Loblolly and shortleaf pines	66.6	2.0	0.0	0.3	24.1	40.1
Cypress	0.1	0.0	0.1	0.0	0.0	0.0
Other eastern softwoods	1.6	0.3	0.0	0.0	0.0	1.3
Total softwoods	68.3	2.2	0.2	0.3	24.1	41.4
Hardwood						
Select white oaks	3.3	0.2	0.0	0.0	0.5	2.6
Select red oaks	2.6	0.0	0.0	0.0	0.1	2.5
Other white oaks	9.4	0.2	1.1	0.2	0.7	7.3
Other red oaks	8.8	0.1	0.0	0.0	0.8	7.9
Hickory	4.3	0.0	0.3	0.1	0.8	3.1
Hard maple	0.1	0.0	0.0	0.0	0.0	0.1
Soft maple	0.1	0.0	0.0	0.0	0.1	0.0
Sweetgum	0.8	0.0	0.0	0.0	0.2	0.6
Tupelo and blackgum	0.2	0.0	0.0	0.0	0.2	0.0
Ash	1.2	0.0	0.1	0.0	0.1	1.0
Cottonwood and aspen	0.0	0.0	0.0	0.0	0.0	0.0
Basswood	0.0	0.0	0.0	0.0	0.0	0.0
Black walnut	0.2	0.0	0.0	0.0	0.0	0.2
Other eastern soft hardwoods	3.8	0.0	0.2	0.0	0.2	3.3
Other eastern hard hardwoods	0.5	0.0	0.0	0.0	0.1	0.5
Eastern noncommercial hardwoods	0.0	0.0	0.0	0.0	0.0	0.0
Other western hardwoods	0.0	0.0	0.0	0.0	0.0	0.0
Total hardwoods	35.2	0.4	1.7	0.3	3.8	29.0
All species	103.5	2.6	1.9	0.7	28.0	70.4

Numbers in rows and columns may not sum to totals due to rounding.

0.0 = no sample for the cell or a value of > 0.0 but < 0.05.

[a] Palm species have been included (species codes 906 to 915).

Table 35.1—Average annual removals of sawtimber on timberland by species group and ownership group, east Oklahoma, 2008 (1993–2008)

Species group[a]	All ownerships	U.S. Forest Service	Other Federal	State and local government	Forest industry	Nonindustrial private
				million board feet[b]		
Softwood						
Loblolly and shortleaf pines	217.1	7.1	0.0	1.8	75.5	132.8
Cypress	0.6	0.0	0.6	0.0	0.0	0.0
Other eastern softwoods	0.0	0.0	0.0	0.0	0.0	0.0
Total softwoods	217.7	7.1	0.6	1.8	75.5	132.8
Hardwood						
Select white oaks	6.8	0.3	0.0	0.0	0.8	5.7
Select red oaks	7.8	0.0	0.0	0.0	0.3	7.5
Other white oaks	11.6	0.3	1.3	0.0	0.9	9.1
Other red oaks	25.0	0.0	0.0	0.0	2.1	22.9
Hickory	8.6	0.0	0.4	0.0	1.3	6.9
Hard maple	0.3	0.0	0.0	0.0	0.0	0.3
Soft maple	0.0	0.0	0.0	0.0	0.0	0.0
Sweetgum	1.9	0.0	0.0	0.0	0.5	1.5
Tupelo and blackgum	0.9	0.0	0.0	0.0	0.9	0.0
Ash	3.8	0.0	0.0	0.0	0.0	3.8
Cottonwood and aspen	0.0	0.0	0.0	0.0	0.0	0.0
Basswood	0.0	0.0	0.0	0.0	0.0	0.0
Black walnut	0.8	0.0	0.0	0.0	0.0	0.8
Other eastern soft hardwoods	7.3	0.0	0.5	0.0	0.2	6.6
Other eastern hard hardwoods	1.5	0.0	0.0	0.0	0.0	1.5
Eastern noncommercial hardwoods	0.0	0.0	0.0	0.0	0.0	0.0
Other western hardwoods	0.0	0.0	0.0	0.0	0.0	0.0
Total hardwoods	76.4	0.6	2.2	0.0	7.1	66.5
All species	294.1	7.6	2.8	1.8	82.5	199.3

Numbers in rows and columns may not sum to totals due to rounding.

0.0 = no sample for the cell or a value of >0.0 but <0.05.

[a] Palm species have been included (species codes 906 to 915).

[b] International ¼-inch rule.

Inventory Methods

Inventory design and methods for collecting and processing forest resource data have changed substantially since the previous east Oklahoma survey in 1992 (methods for this survey were adapted from Rosson and Rose 2010). These changes necessitate the use of caution when making rigorous comparisons between forest resource assessments.

Normally, Forest Inventory and Analysis (FIA) reports the inventory year as the year in which the majority of the plot data collection ended. However, the field work for east Oklahoma, cycle 6 ended in 1992, and the report was titled 1993. For consistency with other States reporting FIA inventory years, the east Oklahoma 2008 report will refer to cycle 6 data as 1992.

The current inventory is a two-phase, fixed-plot design conducted on an annualized basis. Annualized means that a portion of the entire sample population (a cycle) is collected each year until all plots have been measured. Most annualized surveys are conducted over a 5-year period. However, since the east Oklahoma 2008 inventory was a closeout of the old periodic inventory and established the new plot design, plot collection was accelerated and completed in 2 years.

Phase 1 (P1) provides the area estimates for the inventory. Phase 2 (P2) involves on-the-ground measurements of sample plots by field personnel. Phase 3 (P3) is a subset of the P2 plot system where additional measurements are made by field personnel to assess unique forest health indicators, many which are not measured on the P2 plot. Note that P3 plots were not measured for this cycle in east Oklahoma.

Data were processed with the National Inventory and Monitoring System version 4.0 software.

Sample Design Overview: Annual versus Periodic

The current survey's sample design differs in several ways from the one employed previously. One change involved the switch from a periodic survey to an annualized survey. Another involved switching from a variable-radius sample to a fixed-plot sample. These changes, alone or in combination, weaken comparisons between surveys. The only way to quantify the true impact of such changes on trend analysis would be to conduct the survey using both plot designs simultaneously and compare the results of these two independent surveys. Neither the time nor money was available to do this.

Previous surveys of east Oklahoma were periodic; all plots were measured in 1 to 2 years, and the time between remeasurements ranged between 6 to 10 years. The current, annual inventory design was implemented to provide more up-to-date information about forest resources and improved comparability from State to State across the United States. Under the annual inventory system, 20 percent (1 panel) of the total number of plots in a State are measured every year over a 5-year period (1 cycle). Each panel of plots is selected on a subgrid that is slightly offset from the previous panel, so that each panel covers essentially the same sample area (both spatially and in intensity) as the prior panel. In the sixth year, the plots that were measured in the first panel are remeasured. This marks the beginning of the next data-collection cycle. After field measurements are completed, a cycle of data is available for the 5-year report. Because of logistics, economics, and sample implementation protocols, the data set consists of data that are <1-year old (the most recently collected data) as well as data up to 5 years old (the data collected at the beginning of the cycle).

One of the major impacts on data interpretation and analysis of switching to the annual inventory design is the length of time for data collection (5 years versus 1 or 2 years). Data collected over a longer period have a higher probability of sampling a specific event, such as a hurricane or fire, but with only a small proportion of the sample. However, data collected over a shorter time span, such as data collected in the periodic survey, may miss an event entirely until the next periodic measurement takes place, at which time all the sample plots would reflect the event.

Sample Design Phases

The three phases (P1, P2, and P3) of the current sampling method are based on a hexagonal-grid design for sample placement on the ground; successive phases are sampled with less intensity. In general, the P1 phase involves area estimation, the P2 and P3 phases involve placement of sample plots on the ground, where measurement of variable attributes is made. The grid ensures a systematic placement of P2 and P3 plots on the ground. There are 16 P2 hexagons for every P3 hexagon. The P2 hexagons represent approximately 6,000 acres compared to 96,000 acres for the P3 hexagons. To ensure systematic coverage of the sample domain (a State), the goal is to place one P2 plot in every hexagonal grid cell.

Area, current P1—The new approach in the determination of forest area applies a stratification technique to improve the precision of the estimate, in other words, it reduces the variance of the estimate. With this method, the placement (on the ground) and subsequent classification (by land use) of the P2 plot carries much of the weight in determining forest area. The area of control was the survey unit. The Forest Inventory and Analysis (FIA) of the U.S. Department of Agriculture Forest Service Southern Research Station used National Land Cover Data (NLCD) for the stratification platform. The NLCD data has a land classification produced by the U.S. Geological Survey, derived from Landsat Thematic Mapper data. Using these data, FIA protocols identify four strata to improve the variance of the area estimate. These strata are identified by a pixel classification according to four types of placement: (1) pixels in forest, (2) pixels in nonforest, (3) pixels in nonforest but within a 2-pixel width of a forest edge, and (4) pixels in a forest area but within a 2-pixel width of a forest edge. The estimation of forest area is the sum across all strata from respective pixel counts (based on placement within the above strata) and the mean area from the P2 plots. This type of approach places more weight on the P2 plot in area determination than with previous aerial-photo dot count methods.

Area, previous P1—In the 1992 east Oklahoma survey, the estimate of timberland area was based on interpreting dot-grid counts overlaid on recent aerial photographs with each dot classified as forest or nonforest. Each dot represented about 230 acres. The forest or nonforest estimate was then adjusted by ground-truth checks at all permanent sample locations. Permanent sample locations consisted of two types of plots: intensification plots (used only as ground truths for forest and nonforest classifications) and 3- by 3-mile plots (plots on a 3- by 3-mile square grid) where tree measurements and plot characteristics were recorded. The proportion of dots classified as forest was applied to U.S. Census land area data to develop an estimate of forest area in individual counties. Appropriate expansion factors (the timberland area each plot represents) for each forested 3- by 3-mile plot were assigned. The expansion factor was dependent on the number of forested plots in a county, but averaged 5,760 acres per plot for the State. For the dot-count inventories, the area of control was the county (Rosson 2001).

Change in Assessing National Forest and Reserved Lands

Current—Under the annual inventory system, area estimation of all lands and ownerships was based on the probability of selection of P2 plot locations. There was no enumeration of any ownership (no use of known areas of ownership to determine area and plot expansion factors). As a result, the known forest land area (for specific ownerships) does not always agree with area estimates based on probability of selection. For example, the acreage of national forests, published by the U.S. Department of Agriculture Forest Service for the National Forest System, will not agree exactly with the statistical estimate of national forest land derived by FIA. These numbers may differ substantially for very small areas.

Previous—In the 1992 east Oklahoma survey, all national forest lands in a county were enumerated. Additional plots were also added to improve sampling errors. The enumerated or known acreage values were taken from public agency reports and other public domain documents. The enumerated national forest area in each county was divided by the number of sample locations to derive expansion factors. The enumerated forest area values were subtracted from the total forest area derived for the county from P1 estimates, and the remaining forested plots were then divided into the remaining area to derive the expansion factors for the nonenumerated ownerships.

Plot Design

Current P2—Bechtold and Patterson (2005) describe the current P2 and P3 ground plots and explain their use. These plots are clusters of four points arranged so that one point is central and the other three lie 120 feet from it at azimuths of 0, 120, and 240 degrees (fig. B.1). Each point is the center of a circular subplot with a fixed 24-foot radius. Trees ≥5.0 inches in diameter at breast height (d.b.h.) are measured in these subplots. Each subplot in turn contains a circular 1/300-acre microplot

with a fixed 6.8-foot radius (fig. B.2). Trees 1.0 to 4.9 inches in d.b.h. and seedlings (<1.0 inch in d.b.h.) are measured on these microplots.

Sometimes a plot cluster straddles two or more land use or forest condition classes (Bechtold and Patterson 2005). There are seven condition-class variables that require mapping of a unique condition on a plot listed in order of priority:

1. Land use
2. Reserved status
3. Ownership
4. Forest type
5. Stand size
6. Regeneration status
7. Stand density

A new condition is defined and mapped each time the aerial extent of one of these variables is encountered during plot measurement. The process of mapping any of these conditions on a plot changes the plot size for a respective condition, i.e., the condition size will be smaller than a full plot complement, and this may increase the variance of the estimate.

Previous P2—The 1992 inventory of east Oklahoma used a prism sampling design. At each forested location, a sample plot cluster consisting of 10 satellite points was installed. This cluster covered about 1 acre. At each forested sample plot, trees ≥5.0 inches in d.b.h. were selected with a 37.5-basal-area-factor prism at each satellite point. Therefore, each tree selected with the prism represented 3.75 square feet of basal area per acre. Trees ≥1.0, but <5.0 inches in d.b.h. were tallied on a 1/275-acre circular fixed-radius plot (7.1-foot radius) centered at the first three satellite points. Forest conditions were not mapped on the prism 10-point cluster. The land use designation for the entire plot was based on the land use determined at point center of point 1, i.e., if the point center fell on forest land, the entire plot was classified as forest; if the point center fell on a nonforest area, the entire plot was classed as nonforest.

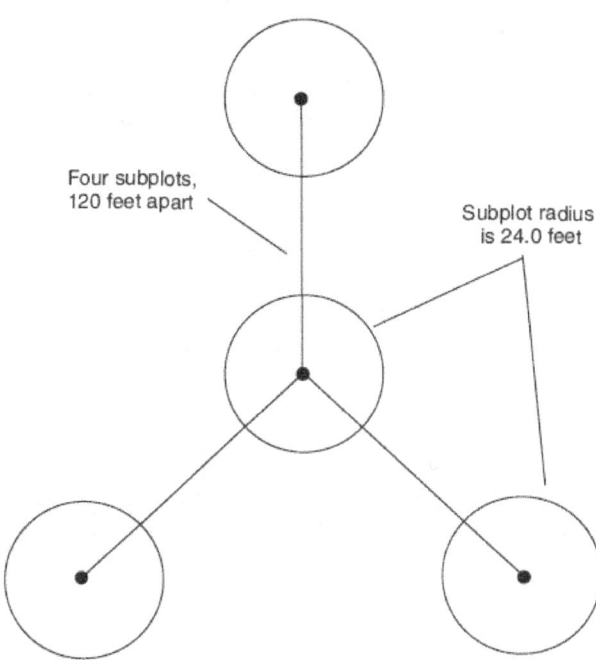

Figure B.1—Annual inventory fixed-plot design (the P2 plot).

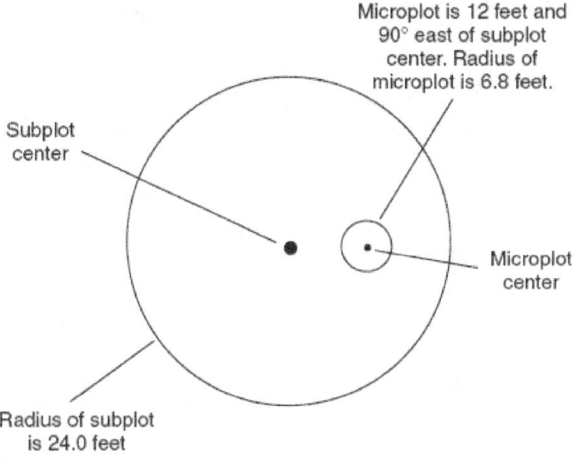

Figure B.2—Subplot and microplot layout.

In situations where point 1 was forested, but portions of the 10-point plot cluster straddled a forest-nonforest area, points that fell in the nonforest area were systematically rotated into the forest area by means of detailed systematic instructions for field crews to ensure that they would rotate points in the same manner for any given situation.

Volume Estimation

Current—Tree volumes for each individual tally tree were derived by a linear regression model. The general form of the model involves two tree measurements from sample trees: d.b.h. and total height. This equation estimated gross cubic-foot volume from a 1-foot stump to a 4-inch upper diameter for each sample tree. Separate equation coefficients for 97 species or species groupings were utilized. The volume in forks in the central bole and the volume in limbs outside of the main bole were excluded. Net cubic-foot volume was derived by subtracting the estimate of rotten or missing wood for each sample tree.

Volume of the saw-log portion (expressed in International ¼-inch board feet) of sample trees was derived by using board foot-to-cubic foot ratio equations. All equations and coefficients were developed from standing and felled tree volume studies conducted by FIA across several Southern States. For more detailed and specific information regarding volume models and coefficients, contact the Southern Research Station, FIA work unit.

Previous—Volumes in the 1992 east Oklahoma survey were derived from measurements of trees on forested sample locations. These deterministic volume measurements included d.b.h., bark thickness, total height, bole length, log length, and four upper-stem diameters (measured with a pentaprism). Smalian's formula was used to compute volume from these measurements. In addition, volume equations were developed to estimate the volume for trees not surviving the measurement period or for past volumes of new sample trees.

It should be noted that a difference in the volume estimation methods discussed above results in a change between the 1992 and 2008 surveys that is due, in large part, to the procedures used, not to real change in the volume. Differentiating the real change in the resource from that due to computational procedures is difficult and results in only an approximation of change. A comparison of the two methods indicates that the volume equations used for the 2008 data results in approximately 5 percent more volume for the total inventory.

Biomass (and Carbon) Estimation

Current—Tree biomass for each individual tally tree was derived by applying models and coefficients derived by McClure and others (1981) and McClure and Knight (1984). The general form of the model utilized two tree measurements from sample trees: d.b.h. and total height. The coefficients derived green weight by means of a volume conversion method. The dry weight was then derived by multiplying the green weight by 0.5. The tree biomass model gives the weight of the total tree, including wood and bark, from ground level; foliage is not included. The model for the merchantable stem, including wood and bark, gives the weight of the stem from a 1-foot stump to a 4-inch top. The biomass estimates in this report were derived with this regional estimator (versus the national component ratio method). For more detailed and specific information regarding biomass models and coefficients, contact the Southern Research Station, FIA work unit.

Previous—Tree biomass for each individual tally tree was derived by applying partitioned models and coefficients by Alexander Clark (Research Forester; U.S. Forest Service, Southern Research Station, Athens, GA). The general form of the model utilized two tree measurements from sample trees: d.b.h. and total height. The coefficients for both dry and green weights were applied to the tree data. The tree biomass models gave the weight, including wood and bark, of all tree components from a 1-foot stump; foliage was not included. The merchantable stem component, including wood and bark, extends from a 1-foot stump to a 4-inch top. See Rosson (2001) for more details of these models.

Growth, Removals, and Mortality Estimation

Growth, removals, and mortality (GRM) estimates were determined from the remeasurement of sample plots measured in the 1992 inventory. Several factors impacted the GRM estimates, especially if comparing these with past surveys of east Oklahoma. First, all of the plots from the 1992 survey were not remeasured because of logistics, economics, and efficiency involving field work. Of the 1,763 timberland plots measured in 1992, 1,073 were remeasured. This weakened reversion and diversion (see definitions in glossary) estimates. Second, only the first 5 points of each 10-point plot were measured (fig. B.3). Third, the Beers and Miller (1964) estimator technique was used to determine gross growth, net growth, removals, mortality, and net change of the inventory. Ingrowth was derived from new trees on the microplot (fig. B.4). This methodology required personnel to account only for previously tallied trees. The 1992 survey utilized the Van Deusen method to derive growth, a method that utilized ongrowth and nongrowth trees (Van Deusen and others 1986). Because of the issues above, GRMs in this report were only reported for plots that were on timberland in 1992 and were still on timberland in 2008. In addition, many of the factors discussed weaken comparisons with past GRM estimates of east Oklahoma.

Data labels on charts and within the text refer to the remeasurement period as 1993 to 2008. This 16-year period represents the beginning year and ending year used to calculate the average annual estimates.

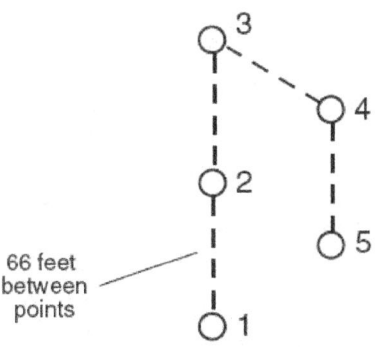

Figure B.3—Configuration of 5-point satellite sample unit (used to collect remeasurement data for growth, removals, and mortality in the 2008 survey).

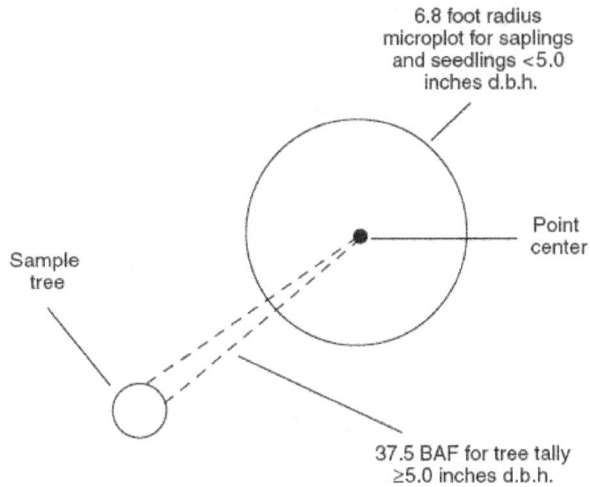

Figure B.4—Configuration of one satellite point.

Changes in Variable Algorithms

The methods used to assess various attributes have also changed and this, too, impacts trend analysis. Three of the more important attributes in the forest survey are stocking, forest type, and stand size. In the 1992 survey, a stocking algorithm was used to determine individual tree stocking and this in turn was used as an importance value in deriving a forest type and stand size for each plot. With the implementation of the new fixed plot sample design, the stocking algorithm changed, along with the forest-type algorithm and stand-size algorithm.

Privacy Laws

It is important that forest landowners and FIA data users understand the Federal statutory requirement that private ownership information collected during an FIA survey shall not be made available for public distribution. In addition, Federal law also requires that the exact locations of all FIA plots shall not be made public and that the ownership of each plot must be masked. This report summarizes FIA data by ownership class at the unit and State levels. Breakout of private ownership information within the county level is no longer permitted on the FIA database Web

site. However, public ownership classes may be summarized at the county level.

Summary

Users wishing to make rigorous comparisons of data among surveys should be aware of the significant differences in plot designs and variable assessments. Assuming there is no bias in plot selection or maintenance of plot integrity, the most valuable and powerful trend information is obtained when the same plots are revisited from one survey to the next and measured in the same way. This is also the only method that yields reliable components of change estimation (GRM) especially by specific attributes such as species. This approach reduces the noise that is present in data for natural forest stands and increases the level of confidence in assessments of trends. However, if sample designs change, there can never be a high level of certainty that the trends in the data are real and not due to procedural changes. Even though both designs may be judged statistically valid, the naturally occurring noise in the data hinders confident and rigorous assessments of trend over time. Determining the strength of a trend, or determining the level of confidence associated with a trend, is difficult or impossible when sampling methods change over time.

Data Reliability

Inventory Quality Assurance and Quality Control

The goal of the U.S. Department of Agriculture Forest Service forest inventory quality assurance (QA) program is to provide a framework to assure the production of complete, accurate, and unbiased forest assessments for given standards. To achieve this goal, the Forest Inventory and Analysis (FIA) Program includes data quality documentation in all nationally available reports, including State reports and national summaries.

This report on east Oklahoma forest resources includes a summary of P2 variables and measurement quality objective (MQO) analyses from FIA blind check measurements. Quality assessments of the P3 data will be addressed in future reports, as these data were not collected during this cycle. Quality control (QC) procedures include feedback to field staff to provide assessment and improvement of crew performance. Additionally, data quality is assessed and documented using performance measurements and postsurvey assessments. These assessments are then used to identify areas of the data collection process that need improvement or refine-ment to meet quality objectives of the program.

Quality Assurance and Quality Control Methods

FIA implements QA and QC methods in several different ways. These methods include nationally standardized field man-uals, portable data recorders, training and certification of field crews, and field audits. The portable data recorders help assure that specified procedures are followed. The minimum national standards for annual training of field crews require: (1) a mini-mum of 40 hours for new employees and (2) a minimum of 8 hours for return employees. Field crew personnel are certified at an in-situ test plot. Each crew is required to have at least one certified person present on the plot at all times.

Field Audits

Hot check—A hot check is an inspection normally done as part of the training process. The inspector is present with crew to document crew performance as they measure plots. The recommended intensity for hot checks is 2 percent of the plots installed.

Cold check—A cold check is done at regular intervals throughout the field season. The crew that installed the plot is not present at the time of inspection and does not know when or which plots will be remeasured. The inspector visits the completed plot, evaluates the crew's data collection, and notes corrections where necessary. The recommended intensity for cold checks is 5 percent of the plots installed.

Blind check—A blind check is a complete reinstallation measurement of a previously completed plot. However, the QA crew remeasurement is done without the previously recorded data. The first measurement of the plot is referred to as the field measurement and the second measurement as the QA measurement. The field crews do not know in advance when or which of their plots will be measured by a QA crew. This type of blind measurement provides a direct, unbiased observation of measurement precision from two independent crews. Plots selected for blind checks are chosen to be a representative subsample of all plots measured and are randomly selected. Blind checks are planned to be within a 2-week window of the field measurement. The recommended intensity for blind checks is 3 percent of the plots installed.

Measurement Quality Objectives

Each variable collected by FIA is assigned a MQO with desired levels of tolerance for data analyses. The MQOs are documented in the FIA national field manual (U.S. Department of Agriculture Forest Service 2004a, 2004b). In some instances the MQOs were established as a "best guess" of what experienced field crews should be able to

achieve with consistency. Tolerances are somewhat arbitrary and were based on the ability of crews to make repeatable measurements or observations within the assigned MQO. Evaluation of field crew performance is accomplished by calculation of the differences between the field crew and QA crew data collected on blind check plots. Results of these calculations are compared to the established MQOs.

In the analysis of blind check data, an observation is within tolerance when the difference between the field crew and QA crew observations do not exceed the assigned tolerance for that variable. For many categorical variables, the tolerance is "no error" allowed, thus only observations that are identical are within the tolerance level.

Sampling Error

Sampling error is associated with the natural and expected deviation of the sample from the true population mean. This deviation is susceptible to a mathematical evaluation of the probability of error. Sampling errors for State totals are based on one standard deviation. That is, there is a 68.27-percent probability that the confidence interval given for each sample estimate will cover the true population mean (table C.1).

The size of the sampling error generally increases as the size of the area examined decreases. Also, as area or volume totals are stratified by forest type, species, diameter class, ownership, or other sub-units, the sampling error may increase

Table C.1—Statistical reliability for east Oklahoma, 2008

Item	Sampling estimate and condfidence interval		Sampling error
			percent
Timberland (*1,000 acres*)	5,103.1	± 85.2	1.67
All live (*million cubic feet*)			
Inventory	5,143.4	± 145.6	2.83
Net annual growth	175.8	± 8.9	5.05
Annual removals	128.8	± 8.7	6.78
Annual mortality	73.4	± 4.6	6.24
Growing stock (*million cubic feet*)			
Inventory	3,698.8	± 130.2	3.52
Net annual growth	139.6	± 7.9	5.63
Annual removals	103.5	± 7.6	7.35
Annual mortality	41.3	± 3.8	9.16
Sawtimber (*million board feet*[a])			
Inventory	12,325.1	± 586.7	4.76
Net annual growth	551.0	± 35.8	6.50
Annual removals	294.1	± 29.0	9.85
Annual mortality	110.1	± 16.0	14.54

[a] International ¼-inch rule.

and be greatest for the smallest divisions. However, there may be instances where a smaller component does not have a proportionately larger sampling error. This can happen when the postdefined strata are more homogeneous than the larger strata, thereby having a smaller variance. For specific postdefined strata the sampling error is available from online retrievals using the Forest Inventory Data Online at: http://199.128.173.26/fido/index.html; or using EVALIDator at: http://apps.fs.fed. us/Evalidator/tmattribute.jsp; or can be calculated using the following formula:

$$SE_s = SE_t \; \frac{\sqrt{X_t}}{\sqrt{X_s}}$$

where

SE_s = sampling error for subdivision of State total

SE_t = sampling error for State total

X_s = sum of values for the variable of interest (area or volume) for subdivision of State

X_t = total area or volume for State

For example, the estimate of sampling error for volume of hardwood live-tree volume on all private timberland is computed as:

$$SE_s = 3.96 \; \frac{\sqrt{5,143}}{\sqrt{2,929}}$$

Thus, the sampling error is 5.25 percent, and the resulting 67-percent confidence interval for hardwood live-tree inventory volume on all private land on timberland is 2,929 million cubic feet ± 153.8 million cubic feet.

Sampling errors obtained by this method are only approximations of reliability because this process assumes constant variance across all subdivisions of totals.

Timber Product Inventory

Estimates of timber product output (TPO) and plant residues were obtained from canvasses (questionnaires) sent to all primary wood-using mills in the State. The canvasses are used to determine the types and amount of roundwood—such as saw logs, pulpwood, poles, etc., received by each mill, the county of origin of the wood, the species used, and how the mills disposed of bark and wood residues. The canvasses are conducted every 2 to 3 years by personnel from the Oklahoma Forestry Services and the FIA unit of the Southern Research Station. These data are used to augment FIA's annual inventory of timber removals by providing the product proportions for that segment of removals that is used for products.

Individual studies are necessary to track trends and changes in product output levels. Industry surveys conducted in 1996, 1999, 2002, and 2005 were used to determine average annual product output for roundwood and plant byproducts. Total product output, averaged over the survey period, is the sum of the volume of roundwood products from all sources (growing stock and other sources) and the volume of plant byproducts, or the mill residues.

The TPO database can be accessed at: http://srsfia2.fs.fed.us/.

Table D.1—Common name, scientific name, and FIA species code of tree species ≥1.0 and ≤5.0 inches in d.b.h. occurring in the FIA sample, east Oklahoma, 2008

Common name	Scientific name	FIA species code	Trees tallied in sample
			number
Ashe juniper	*Juniperus ashei*	61	1
Eastern redcedar	*J. virginiana*	68	480
Shortleaf pine	*Pinus echinata*	110	310
Loblolly pine	*P. taeda*	131	225
Florida maple	*Acer barbatum*	311	13
Boxelder	*A. negundo*	313	36
Red maple	*A. rubrum*	316	204
Silver maple	*A. saccharinum*	317	1
Sugar maple	*A. saccharum*	318	6
Ailanthus	*Ailanthus altissima*	341	3
Mimosa, silktree	*Albizia julibrissin*	345	6
Serviceberry spp.	*Amelanchier spp.*	356	46
Pawpaw	*Asimina triloba*	367	3
River birch	*Betula nigra*	373	6
Chittamwood, gum bumelia	*Sideroxylon lanuginosum*	381	44
American hornbeam, musclewood	*Carpinus caroliniana*	391	28
Water hickory	*Carya aquatica*	401	6
Bitternut hickory	*C. cordiformis*	402	101
Pignut hickory	*C. glabra*	403	30
Pecan	*C. illinoinensis*	404	25
Shagbark hickory	*C. ovata*	407	10
Black hickory	*C. texana*	408	399
Mockernut hickory	*C. alba*	409	382
Allegheny chinkapin	*Castanea pumila*	422	1
Ozark chinkapin	*C. pumila* var *ozarkensis*	423	1
Sugarberry	*Celtis laevigata*	461	153
Hackberry	*C. occidentalis*	462	98
Eastern redbud	*Cercis canadensis*	471	82
Flowering dogwood	*Cornus florida*	491	197
Hawthorn spp.	*Crataegus spp.*	500	63
Cockspur hawthorn	*C. crus-galli*	501	3
Common persimmon	*Diospyros virginiana*	521	189
American beech	*Fagus grandifolia*	531	14
White ash	*Fraxinus americana*	541	218
Green ash	*F. pennsylvanica*	544	283
Honeylocust	*Gleditsia triacanthos*	552	75
American holly	*Ilex opaca*	591	26
Black walnut	*Juglans nigra*	602	5
Sweetgum	*Liquidambar styraciflua*	611	66
Osage-orange	*Maclura pomifera*	641	27
Prairie crab apple	*Malus ioensis*	664	2
Red mulberry	*Morus rubra*	682	21
Blackgum	*Nyssa sylvatica*	693	133

continued

Table D.1—Common name, scientific name, and FIA species code of tree species ≥1.0 and ≤5.0 inches in d.b.h. occurring in the FIA sample, east Oklahoma, 2008 (continued)

Common name	Scientific name	FIA species code	Trees tallied in sample
			number
Eastern hophornbeam	*Ostrya virginiana*	701	149
Water-elm, planertree	*Planera aquatica*	722	2
American sycamore	*Platanus occidentalis*	731	5
Pin cherry	*Prunus pensylvanica*	761	2
Black cherry	*P. serotina*	762	211
American plum	*P. americana*	766	16
White oak	*Quercus alba*	802	168
Southern red oak	*Q. falcata*	812	115
Cherrybark oak	*Q. pagoda*	813	11
Overcup oak	*Q. lyrata*	822	6
Bur oak	*Q. macrocarpa*	823	6
Blackjack oak	*Q. marilandica*	824	321
Swamp chestnut oak	*Q. michauxii*	825	7
Chinkapin oak	*Q. muehlenbergii*	826	40
Water oak	*Q. nigra*	827	206
Texas red oak	*Q. texana*	828	2
Pin oak	*Q. palustris*	830	11
Willow oak	*Q. phellos*	831	18
Chestnut oak	*Q. prinus*	832	3
Northern red oak	*Q. rubra*	833	118
Shumard oak	*Q. shumardii*	834	32
Post oak	*Q. stellata*	835	750
Black oak	*Q. velutina*	837	338
Black locust	*Robinia pseudoacacia*	901	40
Western soapberry	*Sapindus saponaria* var *drummondii*	919	3
Black willow	*Salix nigra*	922	14
Sassafras	*Sassafras albidum*	931	138
Winged elm	*Ulmus alata*	971	1,157
American elm	*U. americana*	972	61
Cedar elm	*U. crassifolia*	973	19
Slippery elm	*U. rubra*	975	65
September elm	*U. serotina*	976	8
Other or unknown live tree	*Tree unknown*	999	2

FIA = Forest Inventory and Analysis.

There were 8,066 trees tallied in this size class. Nomenclature follows Little (1979) and USDA Natural Resources Conservation Service (2006).